FEB 1 0 2011

Withdrawn/ABCL

ONE PAGE AT A TIME

(On a Writing Life)

Pat Carr

Texas Tech University Press

This book is typeset in Weiss. The paper used in this book meets the
minimum requirements of ANSI/NISO Z39.48-1992 (R1997). ⊗

Designed by Kasey McBeath

Library of Congress Cataloging-in-Publication Data
Carr, Pat M., 1932–
One page at a time : on a writing life / Pat Carr.
p. cm.
Summary: "Presented in single-page episodes, this memoir highlights
formative moments of author Pat Carr's life, ranging from childhood
to adulthood, that touch on her role as a writer. Reveals struggles with
her mother, her husband, racial and gender discrimination, and—
above all—her place within the world of professional writers"
—Provided by publisher.
ISBN 978-0-89672-716-8 (hardcover: alk. paper)
1. Carr, Pat M., 1932– —Biography. 2. Authors, American—21st
century—Biography. I. Title.
PS3553.A7633Z46 2010
813'.6—dc22
[B]   2010035080

Printed in the United States of America
10 11 12 13 14 15 16 17 18 / 9 8 7 6 5 4 3 2 1

Texas Tech University Press
Box 41037 l Lubbock, Texas 79409-1037 USA
800.832.4042 l ttup@ttu.edu l www.ttupress.org

To Duane Carr, whose expertise I can't do without, and to Jennie Brown, Stephanie Cohen, Angela Leone, Natalie Reid, and Pat Taylor, whose encouragement was essential

I knew I wanted to be a writer before I learned how to write. Long before I'd mastered the alphabet, I creased scraps of paper into folios lined with squiggles that I could "read" to anyone who would sit still long enough to listen.

I don't remember that either my father or mother ever read aloud to my brother or me, but since I've always loved stories, I may have come to them by way of the movies. Every Saturday, even with a blizzard imminent, my father drove the snow-covered Wyoming road from our little oil camp of Grass Creek to Thermopolis so we could see whatever picture was playing at the one theater in town. My mother said that even at age two, I never fell asleep in a movie.

Or I may have acquired a taste for narratives and dialogue by listening to family programs on the radio every Sunday night. Grass Creek didn't have electricity, so the people in camp used battery-operated radios to hear Jack Benny, Fred Allen, and Lux Radio Theatre, and during the winter as we gathered around the gas heater, reflecting its blue flames from little isinglass squares, cold seeped up through the linoleum and the carpet into our bones. But my brother and I never left the side of the radio until my father turned it off and extinguished the gas lamps that jutted from the walls.

Or perhaps because I was intrigued by the comics of the Sunday *Denver Post*—which arrived at my grandmother's store with the wilting lettuce on Wednesdays—I sat with the newspaper open in my lap and made up stories to fit the illustrations.

Or I may have come to stories simply through the lies the adults in my life told.

2

My grandmother Ellen probably told the most elaborate lies, and I'm certain I got my lifelong interest in the Civil War from her tales.

Not only did she insist you could identify a lady by her narrow feet—and she always let people know that the brown alligator heels she wore were size quadruple A even as she had to cramp her toes into the grotesque overlap of a Chinese woman's bound feet in order to lace them up—but she also told wonderful stories about her aristocratic life on a Southern plantation before the war (the War of Northern Aggression, of course). She told how she and the slaves tied the family sterling in a pillowcase and hung it in the well to save it from Sherman's marauders, and how after the war she rescued the flatware and pawned the serving pieces to escape from her convent school and elope with her sweetheart, a boy from the next war-ravaged plantation.

That marriage was annulled after her father sent his overseer to track down the young couple, and Ellen may have had a second husband with the surname Parker, whom she divorced to go to Wyoming, where she found her third husband, Ed. I always considered Ed my grandfather even though my mother was in high school when Ellen married him. When he died, Ellen married a fourth time, and it was only after she and that last one—ironically named "Sherman"—were dead that I discovered her birth certificate, which revealed she'd been born in Big Muddy, Texas, but not until 1876.

I suppose she didn't know enough about Custer to have invented the story that her father died at Little Bighorn and that she'd been born to his widow, but of course the Civil War had more potential for romance anyway.

Ellen, like Ed, presumably wasn't related to any of us, and the story my mother, Bea, told was that Ellen had been the midwife at the bedside of a girl who glanced at her newborn and said, "I don't want it. Take it away or I'll throw it in the street." I heard the story so often I was convinced—and rather relieved, since Ellen's jaw rarely unclenched from a ridge of anger or her eyebrows from a juncture of wrath at the bridge of her nose—that Ellen wasn't my mother's birth mother.

She and Bea agreed on the midwife story, and I'm sure it gave me a writer's fascination with abandonment, but now I'm no longer sure they weren't related. They had the same taste in clothes, food, and china—which they bought in matching sets for twelve so they could serve twenty-four at bridge where they showed off their brilliance at cards. They insisted upper-class women should wear only fourteen-karat gold or platinum, that their furs be beaver or mink, and that ladies should sparkle and blink carefully tended lashes, particularly at men. Those preferences, of course, could stem from the fact that the two of them lived together until Bea left for high school, but since they also shared chestnut hair, the same high cheekbones, the same lemon-pulp irises, and the same delicate long bones, I've begun to wonder whether the midwife story wasn't just another invention Ellen told Grass Creek bachelors to explain why she'd come dragging a child to an oil boomtown.

Nor am I certain Bea didn't cling to the story for its romantic, rebel image. She always insisted she rejected her wealthy "real" parents—second-generation Irish Americans of the rich Moody clan from Galveston—to stay with Ellen.

My father, who'd possibly also been abandoned, wanted to be a writer, and he had a cardboard box of manuscripts on the shelf above his starched white shirts. He never let anyone read the stories he'd written, but I'm sure they were as colorful as Bea's and Ellen's since the version of his life I heard growing up was that his mother, Nella May, and my grandfather Luther Moore, a blacksmith, divorced when my father was seven. They had four daughters and one son, so each took two girls and left the little boy on a street corner in a little Kentucky town. According to his story, he knocked around, graduated from high school at thirteen, and then hitchhiked to Wyoming where he slept in silos ("You stay warm if you burrow in the grain.") until he ended up in Grass Creek with a distant relative, Mac, who owned the town's one grocery store. My father bunked under the counter beside the canned peaches.

That Oliver Twist element reinforced my interest in orphan pluck, but the actual story—related by a Kentucky cousin years later—may have been that Nella had an affair with the hired man, and that Luther came home from the field one afternoon (so maybe he wasn't a blacksmith) to find them in bed. Brandishing a pitchfork, Luther chased the hired man into the next county. (A pitchfork, cracked into three pieces and tied with a frayed rope, lies in the cousin's attic.) When Nella May left, she evidently took her little boy with her. And it turns out that my father probably didn't graduate from high school but that he left school around the sixth grade to go with his mother to Wyoming.

Even as a child, I suspected the silo and the store shelf might have been slightly exaggerated, but, of course, they were the stuff of terrific fiction.

Ellen had evidently been sleeping with Mac, both living in Grass Creek, Wyoming, by now, and about the time Mac rescued my father from the silo (if there was one), she decided it was time for them to marry. When he refused, she, out of spite, married a roustabout immigrant from Germany, Ed Schroeder, who wore diamond rings on both hands and who may (or may not) have been an officer in the Kaiser's army during World War I. But while Ellen used Ed's diamonds to buy the store out from under Mac, she despised her third husband, and she mocked his heavy German accent and always referred to him as "that old fool."

I blamed her for her cruelty to him, and even though he reeked of Meerschaum pipe tobacco and the bologna he sliced at the meat counter, I always tried to spend more time with him than with her. During the Depression when he herded sheep to help float the store, I liked visiting him out on the prairie, where we ate rattlesnake shish kebabs and raisin pie, much better than I liked being in her kitchen behind the store, where she served elaborately frosted, swirled-with-rainbow-colors, angel food cake.

Of course, I may also have held it against her that she made no secret of her preference for my older brother. She complimented Mike's intelligence, his straight little back, his handsomeness, and if my mother asked, "Don't you think Pat's pretty, too?" Ellen's scowl would deepen, and she'd mutter, "Pretty is as pretty does."

I must have been jolted the first time I heard that, but she repeated it often enough to convince me that actions spoke louder than looks, and as a result I realized that if I never had to compete in the beauty market, I could avoid my mother's rigid girdle, her gummy lipstick, and I could concentrate on what I wanted to do, what I wanted to write.

A natural separation existed in my mind between the "true" stories my mother, grandmother, and father told and the "made-up" movie plots we saw each Saturday.

During the week, if the temperature hit at least 30°, I'd bundle up and sit on the porch swing to review the film we'd seen in Thermopolis the previous weekend. Swaying back and forth with the wooden slats nauseated me, so I always banished Mike from the swing and insisted on sitting motionless and alone in the still air.

My view from the porch across the dirt road was my father's office, but since I was nearsighted, I substituted a scrim of images from the movie for the hazy yellow buildings and the fuzzy yellow car barn. By Tuesday, however, I'd repeated the scenes and dialogue to ragged sufficiency, and by Wednesday I'd start making up my own narratives. My settings sprang full-blown from the urban streets—usually New York's—I'd seen on the screen, and my stories generally contained snippets of city adventures.

I preferred romantic comedies, but of course I replicated any movie the theater showed. Occasionally we saw a James Cagney gangster film, but since my little Irish father strongly resembled the Irish Cagney, who always shot someone in the first reel and had to die by the last reel, I generally avoided inventing crime stories. Although I did notice that the young lovers got together after Cagney died (which he did with impressive staggering and gurgling) and that everything turned out all right, I nonetheless felt uncomfortable allowing a character who had a pug nose like my father (although not the black hair slicked with Brilliantine into shiny patent leather) to die in the gutter, and I thus found it more satisfactory to create my happy endings pure.

There also seemed to be a distinction between what passed for truth in my family and fairy tales and myths. I couldn't quite willingly suspend my disbelief for the brothers Grimm or the children's version of the Greek gods and goddesses that came with the encyclopedia my father bought from a door-to-door salesman who'd once wandered through Grass Creek, but one myth, that of Santa Claus, was hard to avoid. All the adults in the oil camp—even Ed, who nodded a yellow-toothed grin while he mispronounced the name—told us about Santa and urged Mike and me to believe in his magical story.

And we did believe. At least until my fourth Christmas Eve.

My father was helping us hang our stockings on the back of a chair beside the Christmas tree—whose illumination came from silver foil icicles and glass balls reflecting the wavering flames of the gas lights—when all at once he tilted his head and whispered, "Listen! Do you hear that? I think it's Santa's sleigh bells."

We paused and could indeed detect a jingle jangle of bells outside in the snow. Mike's eyes opened hugely as my father added, "I bet that's Santa coming now."

The bells rang cheerfully for another few seconds. Then we heard a loud thud, and all sound stopped before a voice sputtered, "Damnation!"

My father didn't try to explain the all-too-familiar curse echoing from the snow darkness, and a minute later when my mother limped in the back door and wiped sheep pellets—laid down for next spring's garden—from her chin with a furious, "I tripped over the gas pipe," my father didn't try to explain that either.

8

Fortunately, I was able to avoid all the supernatural elements—and allusions—associated with organized religion.

Our isolated oil camp—about as close to the middle of nowhere as anyone could get—had no extra cash to support a church or a regular minister during the hard times of the Depression, so my father—as camp boss—allowed the two-room, weekday schoolhouse to serve as a Sunday church. He often snagged a circuit-riding preacher on his way to Cody or Powell (sometimes a Baptist, sometimes a Methodist, and once even a pair of Mormon missionaries) to stop by. But on the Sundays when no minister appeared, my father himself acted as emcee. He actually believed in Fate and cosmic planning ("That's what was supposed to happen."), but he never imposed his fatalism on Grass Creek, and in the adults' room he let Fat Smotherman explain the Bible and let Shorty Gordon sing gospel songs while the elementary teacher, Miss Lee, played the rickety piano.

In the children's room, my mother spread a tablecloth over the teacher's desk, crouched down, and used homemade sock puppets to tell stories about Jesus, Jonah, and Noah—deepening her voice to fit the all-male casts—but their fabulous exploits often seemed to me suspiciously close to those of Santa or Zeus.

Ellen's elopement narrative had involved escaping a convent, but she never mentioned religion or closed the store on Sundays to come to the school/church. My mother kept saying she might pick a religion one day—the Mormon boys were her favorite traveling ministers—but she never did.

And she never imposed the rigors of church doctrine on Mike or me.

I often think that a childhood spent observing my parents' disparate styles convinced me that everyone is unique.

My father was calm, and since he often carried me as a baby to his office, I may have soaked up his tranquility as I lay in a basket beside his desk. He thought things out and solved problems with a quiet "Let's talk"—whether he was in the office after Les Nickels caused a tank spill or at home after Mike head-butted J.W. in the stomach. (J.W. had teased him and my father had said, "You can stop it. Just use your head.")

My mother, on the other hand, commanded with gelid silence. If one of us broke a rule or hurt her feelings by not paying strict attention when she talked, she retreated from volubility into icy disapproval and donned a frigid layer of injury that became a cloak of invisibility in which she didn't disappear but the rest of us did.

I probably admired equally his determined rationality and her steely control, but since her disappointments were more unequivocal, I spent more time placating her.

I often had nosebleeds at night, however, and if I awoke to a bloody pillow, I had to pad across the frozen linoleum and bother her. She'd light the gas lamp in the bathroom and go back to bed while I sat on a high stool and leaned over to watch great scarlet drops fall from my nose and splatter like overripe berries against the curve of the basin. If I fell asleep, my blood would clot and stopper my nostrils, and I'd wake up struggling for air. In my half-asleep grogginess, I'd blow my nose so I could breathe, and the bleeding would start again. If my mother got up and found me still bleeding, her silence would be as cold as the white enameled iron sink.

The land itself undoubtedly contributed to my becoming "someone on whom nothing is lost" because in such a vast and barren hard-scrabble place of sagebrush and rattlesnakes, everyone had to pay attention. Anyone who misjudged snow clouds could get caught in a blizzard; anyone who startled a rattler could get bitten. Everyone had to gauge the sky and ground and mustard yellow office buildings and mustard yellow company houses that huddled beneath corroded metal skeletons of oil rigs. No one could ignore the jack rods that pumped constantly back and forth, grooving the dirt with an animal whine while endless pipelines curved through the arid ravines until their rusting joints and elbows disappeared into the foothills.

The rainbow slick of the sump hole at the end of the line of tanks usually held the stiff, upturned legs of a cow or sheep or deer that had slipped into the black pool and had to be lassoed and pulled to the bank—always too late. Odors of oil and the natural gas burning in a flare beside the post office clamped like a lid over the minuscule town and clung to school sweaters and Big Chief tablets. The flavor of crude could be detected in Sunday apple pies and in the radishes from spring gardens.

And by the end of summer, when the sun beat down from a relentlessly empty sky, the alkaline water dried in concentric white rings at the base of the cottonwood tree by the bridge across the creek bed. After the last puddle vanished, the ground split into the dry, baked fissures of overdone cake.

As much as my mother fascinated me, I didn't use her as a character in my mental narratives. Perhaps because she was already larger than life, I wasn't certain how to change her into fiction. Or perhaps it was because she'd already fabricated herself, and I couldn't enlarge on her invention. At any rate, she never had even a bit part in my stories.

She admitted to being born in 1906, two years before my father—making her a rare 1920s wife older than her husband—but apparently that age wasn't quite accurate, and I once found a snapshot of a girl possibly four or five, inscribed, "Bea, 1906."

Another rarity was that she also stood two inches taller than my father. She obviously disliked the fact that my father was short, and she tried to limit photographs to the pair of them seated. If forced to pose in outdoor lighting, she usually found a hollow to step into. When she stood next to my father, she leaned against him and laid her head on his shoulder to appear his size. But she always seemed uncomfortable touching anyone—even in photographs— and while he obviously adored her, it was far from certain to me that she even liked him.

She'd married using "Parker," and since she insisted that an assumed name voided the marriage (Ellen had never provided adoption papers), she milked the part of being an elegant mistress. She shopped for fashionable dresses and high heels in Thermopolis, and she demanded that my father produce gold watches or platinum hearts circled with diamond chips on Christmas and birthdays. As she unwrapped his presents, she'd glance at him archly and murmur that if he continued to watch himself, she might consider marrying him some day.

While I strove to separate kindness from cruelty and indifference, I saw in Ed the one person in my childhood who seemed to enjoy physical contact. Whenever my mother and I came into the rooms behind the store, his crumpled face wrinkled with pleasure, and he always lumbered up from the rocking chair between the radio and the window to embrace us even if we'd seen him just the day before.

He was the one person I knew who listened to the radio on weekdays, and the only one, besides me, who found snakes fascinating. He could expound for an hour, or until Ellen interrupted with an order, on snakes, and while he didn't actually say it, he left the impression he'd personally handled cobras and vipers. He said a rattlesnake would do almost anything to avoid sinking its fangs into a human being. Reptilian jaws couldn't open wide enough to swallow even a small child, and if a snake used up its venom, it'd be helpless for six weeks. "People let them alone, they let people alone," he'd repeat with his Teutonic accent while he nodded sagely.

He liked ice cream, and even if I wasn't fond of it, when Mike and I went with my father to the pool hall—the only place in town to buy comic books or vanilla ice cream—I'd walk across the dirt road to Ellen's store with a cone for me and one for Ed. The two of us would sit outside on the back steps while melting cream dripped off our fingers, and when he finished his cone, I always gave him the rest of mine.

I loved that he was affectionate, but his need to hug and to take my hand in his blue-veined one when we strolled outside made him as vulnerable as the other people in my life, and I always felt obligated to protect his feelings, too.

In the bleakest days of the Depression, my father decided to go to California. He wasn't, of course, like the hollow-cheeked hobos passing through Thermopolis on boxcars and looking for work; in fact, he was one of two men in Grass Creek who actually had a job. But because Standard Oil reduced its operation, he decided that he, my mother, Mike and I, and Ellen—whom he didn't care for, but who would be company for Bea—could spend the summer beside the ocean.

He told us of the plan in December, and I felt as if I'd been anticipating June for years until at last he drove us to Denver and bought our train tickets.

Then he went back to Grass Creek to pack up our Buick for his drive across half the continent.

I'd seen trains in the movies, and as we left the station I tried to make up stories about Hollywood stars on their way to Las Vegas. But as sage, cottonwoods, and the baked countryside continued to slide behind our Pullman car that rattled, clanged, and clattered along the rails while the engine whistled and hissed steam when the train paused, I decided trains were too noisy for creativity.

I remember Ellen calling the porter in his red uniform "a colored man."

When my mother requested that he put a bag on a shelf, and she tipped him and said, "Thank you, George," Mike wanted to know if she knew him.

She snapped her purse shut. "Oh, they're all named George."

My father had rented rooms for us in a tourist court on Venice Beach, and when he joined us in California, we all crowded into the little rooms with luggage and the new matching shorts and shirts (blue for Mike, red for me) that my mother had decided we needed for a summer by the sea.

Possibly it was sitting on the beach in deck chairs and watching the white-crested, turquoise Pacific waves that triggered my parents' asking me for the first time, "If we all were on a ship and it sank and you could save one of us, which one would you save?"

I looked up from the sand castle Mike and I were building, and as I studied their faces, I knew with sudden sun-glancing-blindingly-off-the-water awareness that I'd somehow been appointed guardian of their feelings. If I chose my mother, my father would be crushed; if I chose him, she'd be destroyed. So I packed a fistful of moist sand onto the sand tower and murmured, "I guess I'd have to save Mike."

They waited a few days to ask again, and when I gave them the same response, I knew they'd ask again. With as much certainty as I knew my new red wool swimsuit would be itchy, I knew they craved my approval. But I'd also realized they could never make me answer.

I don't remember how many times in my childhood they posed that shipwreck scene, but years after they asked for the first time, when my little sister Honey was born, I could switch from saving Mike to rescuing the baby from a watery grave.

Until at last they gave up.

Early snapshots of Mike with me showed him circling an arm protectively around me, the sixteen-months-younger sister. But that summer in California, our roles reversed.

We went every day to the beach with our set of tiny metal cars, and often a boy from the neighborhood would lope across the sand in his bathing trunks to join us. He was a gawky boy, his eyes faded by the sun glare on the waves, who brought a marvelous California toy, a tin gas station, for us to use with our cars.

A two-foot square of enameled lawns and flowerbeds, it had tin streets leading to the gaily enameled tin cube of a station flanked by two meticulously painted tin gas pumps. After we positioned the metal square, we could build a vast array of sand houses and streets beyond the hub of the station, and I could make up characters to live in the town.

The pale-eyed boy always demanded the best cars as he added, "If I can use the tow truck today, I'll give you the station when we're through playing."

But somehow, every day, Mike ended up offending the boy, who retrieved his toy while he kicked apart our beach-front property and stalked away. "I was going to give you my filling station, but now I'm not going to."

Mike always muttered forlornly, "He'd have given me the station if I hadn't driven my car over his yard." Or occasionally, "I don't think he liked your story."

I was five and I didn't recognize his entrenched seven-year-old innocence until I'd cautioned three or four times, "He wasn't going to give you the station. He always finds excuses not to. He won't ever give it to you."

But Mike always looked sadly after the boy. "He will if we don't make him mad."

I observed my paternal grandmother, Nella May—
the one person besides my parents and Mike I was positive-
ly related to—only once. One weekend during that same
California summer, we left Ellen in the Venice Beach cabin
while my father drove the rest of us to Seattle to visit Nella
and her second—or perhaps third—husband.

My mother pulled the address from her lizard-skin purse
as we stopped beside a large white two-story house. "Yes.
This should be it."

A huge tree, its branches drooping ripe cherries, stood
in the front yard, and my father, almost dainty at five
foot seven, looked even slighter as he passed beneath the
boughs glistening with bright red fruit and glossy green
leaves.

He reached the front porch, but before he could climb
the steps, an obese woman in a zeppelin-sized print dress
and apron swung the door back and loomed in the opening.
She glared down at him in his white shirt with polished hair
and shoes. "Did you lose your job, Stanley? If you're coming here to see if we can put you up, we don't have room."

He assured her he still had a job, that we'd come for a
visit, and although she glowered as we got out of the car,
she moved heavily into the shadowed hall and motioned
with a bloated hand. "You may as well stay for supper then.
It's ready."

I don't remember that she spoke a word to either Mike
or me, but I remember her massive jiggling bare arms—
thicker than my body—as she forked up whole boiled potatoes and great slabs of beef from the platter she used for
a plate. She probably didn't weigh the four or five hundred
pounds I assumed she did, but I always pictured her as the
smeared illustration outside the carnival tent advertising the
fat lady exhibit.

Mrs. Henry was a Grass Creek neighbor who became a symbol in our house and whose Scrooge-like parsimony I used over and over in stories.

Since Mr. Henry was the other man besides my father who'd kept his job in the mustard yellow offices throughout the 1930s, Mrs. Henry could have worn stylish clothes like my mother and could, like my mother, have served her potato soup in gold-rimmed china soup plates. But whenever I overheard her conversations, her topic was always how much she'd saved from Mr. Henry's paycheck. "This Depression don't show signs of letting up. You got to put something back for a rainy day."

I didn't know what rain on our dry hills had to do with anything, but I did know that Mrs. Henry made sheets from stitched-together feed sack squares and turned her cotton dresses inside out every few scrubbings to even the fading of the interior and exterior print. She also wore her husband's hand-me-down gray cardigan with moth-chewed sleeves and his holes-in-the-soles oxfords—without laces—when she clumped along the wooden sidewalk.

My mother, of course, never considered saving a virtue, and she preferred strawberries out of season and liked Whitman's chocolates better on nonholidays. She accepted as her due every ruby or sapphire brooch from my father, and after Mrs. Henry abruptly died one winter Monday while her wash froze on the clothesline, my mother used her as an example of what not to be, always concluding, "She should at least, just once, have bought herself a pair of high heels."

My mother threw Mike an unheard-of celebration for his eighth birthday, a party in Thermopolis for half a dozen children, five little boys and me.

At the one restaurant in town, my father ordered us all the standard haddock smothered in bilious yellow cream gravy and served with mashed potatoes and a tiny dish of iceberg lettuce slick with French dressing. For dessert we had chocolate cake (My mother jammed a tilted birthday candle in Mike's slice.) before we trooped through the snow to the theater to see *Heidi*, which just happened to be playing that weekend.

My mother hugged her beaver coat tighter and nodded her feathered cloche toward the marquee. "*Heidi* is perfect for a children's party. It's from a famous children's book, so I know you'll like it."

She was wrong.

Halfway through the movie, Mike became hysterical over Heidi's trials—culminating in her separation from her grandfather and the smashing of her glass snow globe, whose flakes had once floated lovingly toward a Swiss chalet—and my father had to take him to the lobby to recover. Jack and Murray Cameron wept in the seats beside me, and Danny Delaney, sobbing, climbed into my mother's lap and said through his sobs, "I don't like this story, Mrs. Moore."

I don't know if it was the overwhelming sadness of the film or the fact that the ultimate happy ending—Heidi's reunion with her grandfather—didn't make up for the traumas little Shirley Temple underwent for ninety minutes, but from the night of that gala birthday party, I never quite trusted children's literature.

No girls my age lived in either the Standard Oil camp my father ran or in the Sinclair camp below the pool hall and Ellen's store, so I climbed the dry foothills, looking for agates and arrowheads, with a troop of little boys: Mike, Danny, Jack, and Murray, and occasionally Danny's little brother, Bugs.

Danny watched me with constant adoration and anticipated what I might want. He always gave me any special agate he found even as he gazed at it with longing. If we rode bicycles (Mike's and mine new, Danny's a rusted hand-me-down), Danny would push his bicycle up a hill, then race back for mine.

Whenever we went hiking, I ignored Mike's request for jelly and packed the peanut butter sandwiches plain because I disliked the cloying grit of my mother's gooseberry jam, and I chose the path through the sagebrush and around the slumbering rattlesnakes—with Danny at my heels.

Mike, whom I did let carry the mason jar of water and the tin lunch pail, would often ask wistfully as he followed me, "How come we always do what you want to do?"

I'd learned by then not to try to explain to him, and I didn't say it was because I knew where I wanted to go and what I wanted to do and they could never decide. I didn't say that since Ed had told me that snakes didn't want to be helpless for six weeks, I could notice and choose a path around coiled rattlers better than they could. "Just keep walking. They rattle so we'll leave them alone."

Nor did I say it was because I was a girl and girls were always in charge.

In 1930s Wyoming, no woman could hire out as a roustabout or wildcatter, and even as my mother insisted she rebelled against social restraints, she and Ellen agreed that the acceptable role for a woman was that of wife, mother, nurse, or grade school teacher while the man brought home sufficient cash—and pork—to keep her in a comfortable, if not a lavish, style.

I'd watched Bea and Ellen dominate everyone in camp, and I knew from my own experience how much power girls had, but when I surveyed the other women in Grass Creek, I often wondered at what point most adult females had had to relinquish their control.

When did they have to give up their independence and start flattering?

When did they start fluttering those lacquered eyelashes and manipulating other people—particularly men—to get what they wanted?

When did they have to *marry* "a good provider" rather than providing for themselves?

And since every weekend on the theater screen I saw that men had most of the fun and all the rewards, when I sat on the wooden porch swing and daydreamed adventure stories, my protagonists were always male.

Without knowing it, I'd acquiesced to gender roles.

And for far too many years, my stories would reflect that capitulation.

But I could never make peace with the class system.

Every kid with a father laid off during the Depression was dirt poor, but Danny was possibly poorer than the others. He brought lunch to school only twice a week, but on the days he sat at his desk with folded hands, he nonetheless refused to accept half my sandwich. ("I had a big breakfast with bacon and two eggs. I'm not hungry.")

Miss Lee had assigned him a seat in the last row, and I could glance back and tell he was hungry and cold. All of us were cold, of course, since no matter how much wood Miss Lee piled into the pot-bellied stove, the room stayed frigid, and only at Friday recess, when she lit the incinerator to burn trash, did we get really warm.

All of us had been cautioned not to touch the pilot light, and we were told that, accidental or not, anyone who ignited the fire would be expelled. So the afternoon Jimmy Gleason found a scrawny calico cat hiding in the frozen buffalo grass along the creek, we stood stunned as he flung it into the incinerator and raced to turn on the gas.

Danny, the only one of us who didn't stare dumbfounded, left my side, ran to the iron receptacle, and jumped onto the rusted edge to grab the cat just as Jimmy turned the lever. Blue orange flames roared across the interior. Danny fell back, forehead burned, hair and eyebrows seared off, but the cat sprang clear and sped away.

We stood gaping and shivering while Miss Lee bundled Danny into her car.

The next time I saw him, his face smeared with black crankcase grease, I knew he was smiling at me the way he always did. And when he returned to school, he had no burn scars and was as handsome as ever.

Danny's rescue of the cat stirred me deeply (My husband once said, only half joking, "No woman should ever have a Danny Delaney in her childhood."), and I'd heard the story about how my father, walking an icy pipeline and trying to save a doe from a pond, had broken his leg. With no other recourse, he'd made a cottonwood crutch and hobbled back to camp. I'd witnessed Danny's act and I saw the cast of my father's kind—and physically demanding—effort. But it took the British adventure film *Four Feathers* to complete my hazy definition of heroism and imprint me, like a newly hatched duck, with a narrative model I never escaped.

In the movie, the protagonist, Harry Faversham, re-ceives a white feather, the symbol for a coward, from three friends and his sweetheart, and despite the fact that he's an idealist and a pacifist, he goes to the Anglo-Egyptian war to return the feathers to his friends. To disguise himself as a member of a marked tribe and cross hostile Egypt to find the English army, he submits to being branded on the forehead. After this brave sacrifice, he manages, with inge-nious daring—and a good deal of coincidence—to save his soldier friends and rewin the girl.

Four Feathers set the standard.

While it reaffirmed the reasons I admired my father and Danny, it also demanded that men be heroes. At the time I didn't insist that females be heroic, but after seeing that English movie, I wanted men to be, like Harry Faversham, romantic, kind, intelligent, and strong enough to endure a red-hot iron.

One afternoon while I ate ice cream with Ed, Mike discovered at the pool hall a new comic book featuring the adventures of Superman. Comic books held only mild fairy-tale interest for me, but Mike highly recommended that one, so I dutifully read it.

I didn't mind Superman's extraterrestrial powers or his ability to catch bullets as if they were moths and leap tall buildings in a single bound, but those qualities had no basis in actuality, so I couldn't admire them. Or use them in my own imagined stories.

In 1939, as war swept across Europe and Hitler and Stalin signed a joint nonaggression pact, one of the issues of *Superman Comics* showed the ultimate hero flying (arms and legs in blue tights straight out and red cape flapping) to Germany, swooping into the Reichstag, grabbing Hitler, and then flying on to Russia where he plucked Stalin from the Kremlin. He banged the leaders' heads together— making their comic book eyes into dizzily crossed Xs—and sped back to Europe with a dictator dangling from each hand. In one strong-armed moment, he'd ended the whole European conflict.

Even in the second grade, I didn't approve of such a cavalier attitude toward history. Everyone knew from daily radiocasts and weekly newsreels that Hitler still directed the Nazi war machine, that Stalin ruled Russia, and that Panzer divisions still occupied Poland. I had rather un-willingly suspended my disbelief for Superman's made-up actions occurring in made-up cities, but when the creators used real people in real countries—with fake results—I could no longer even enjoy the plots.

I required heroism, but it had to be believable heroism.

Bea, of course, also set a standard, but hers defined how one should behave in public. Even if it lacked the emotional investment I had in heroism, it did have such a strong aesthetic component I could never quite shake it either.

She filled our yellow company house with antiques, bought tintypes at junk shops to pass off as ancestors ("Who knows? They might be related to me."), and so thoroughly abhorred grape bunches with picked-off grapes ("It's simply bad manners to leave those ugly stems.") that years later, my sister was still giving me grape shears for Christmas.

Bea constantly revised her background, and by the time I was in the fourth grade she was telling strangers she came from Denver rather than from Big Muddy, Texas. This invention did have a few grains of truth since when she'd finished grade eight—the last grade of Grass Creek's school—she went to Denver and worked her way through high school as a maid, or as she said, an "au pair."

In the upper-class households, she'd served daily meals and party dinners on Wedgwood china and sterling flatware, observed aristocratic behavior, and decided that her children would learn to eat soup correctly while they kept their napkins in their laps and their elbows off the table. Since it was also trashy behavior to lift a fork before everyone had been served—even when the table was a plank held up by sawhorses on the Fourth of July—I never bit into a picnic hot dog or a gravy-slathered slice of holiday turkey that hadn't become stone cold.

The Christmas before the United States entered the war, my father drove us to Denver again, this time to view trees in the parks strung with colored bulbs and to let my mother buy buckle shoes and gowns she could wear in Wyoming winters only once or twice a decade. While she shopped, my father took Mike and me to movies.

Denver, a town with glorious abundance, had a street lined with theaters that opened at ten o'clock in the morning, so we started with Laurel and Hardy. When that slapstick comedy let out, we sauntered two doors down to a Fred Astaire and Ginger Rogers musical. I liked realism, and it seemed downright silly for people to tap dance or burst into song in a bank, but I'd realized by then that even though my father wasn't all that enthusiastic about movies, he did like musicals. So before Mike urged us to move on, I decided my father deserved a film he liked, and I insisted we see that one.

We consumed popcorn and pink bonbons during the next film, a romantic comedy, before we went to a cheaper theater on a side street where a Charlie Chan mystery doubled with a Gene Autry western. After we met my mother and ate Swiss steak at the restaurant in the Brown Palace Hotel, my mother decided Mike and I should see *Pinocchio* while she and my father went to *Reap the Wild Wind* three theaters away. I'd rather have seen the adventurous adult movie, but I didn't argue.

Fortunately, *Pinocchio* was short, so I persuaded Mike to go to the other theater where I told the usher we had parents inside. He stared at my red coat, tam, and white cotton stockings and hesitated, but at last he let us in, and we saw nearly the entire movie.

It was the one time in my life I managed to cram seven movies into one day.

In the countdown to the war everyone knew was coming, my father longed to join the army. But since he worked in the oil industry—or possibly couldn't produce a high school diploma—the army refused him. The recruiters sent wildcatters home, too, of course (so maybe the "vital industry" excuse was valid), and even the most militant roustabout had to be satisfied being trained to spot enemy aircraft. But since a single-engine plane flying over the empty hills was such a rare spectacle that Shorty Gordon, high in a rig, and all of us in morning spelling class, even Miss Lee, dropped everything to watch it disappear into the endless sky, no one ever suggested air-raid practice.

My father also hated firearms, so it was probably just as well the army didn't induct him. Although most men in camp kept a rifle to kill snakes or wolves, my father said if the dog couldn't protect himself against prowling coyotes he should stay in the yard, and he said that a hoe was more effective than a shotgun to stop the rattlers that tried to slither under our front porch.

But when the sheriff in Meteesee called (One ring on the phone meant someone wanted the office, two meant our house, and three rings got the store.) to say that while the East Coast was vulnerable to an attack from Germany, the oil reserves in Wyoming might be too, my father accepted a Colt .22 revolver to help protect the camp.

The little gun, with its ridged silver stock that just fit my hand, had a delicious menace along with a hint of mystery and adventure, but my father never let me do anything except hold it, and I got to do that only twice, since after it was stolen from the glove compartment by a hitchhiker, my father never replaced it.

After Pearl Harbor, we Grass Creek children proudly shouted the pledge of allegiance, wore tiny flag pins in our lapels, bought savings stamps at ten cents each, and sorted through the splintered furniture, wagon wheels, and rotting work boots of the dump to lug metal scrap up to the camp office. In the dirt street we erected great towers of rusted iron that could be trucked to Thermopolis.

Those activities couldn't contain our boundless patriotism, however, and one afternoon while my mother was at Ellen's, I remembered the plate in my closet. The delicate porcelain glittered with a scene of Japanese ladies in red kimonos at tea under a crouching tree. But MADE IN JAPAN had been stamped in red on the plate's underside, so I got it from the closet and took it out to where the boys waited.

They looked at me dubiously, but before Mike could decide that whatever plan I had might mean trouble, I lifted the plate and smashed it against the iron garden fence. It shattered into pieces. As I solemnly picked a piece up and dropped it in the drainage pipe, I wanted to make a significant declaration like "Thus to all Japanese," but I felt foolish mouthing something so pompous, so I merely fed china fragments, silently, one by one, into the pipe. After watching a while, the boys began dropping pieces in, too.

Finally the shards were gone, and everyone but Danny went back to the porch.

Just as I turned to join them, I saw a last piece on the ground. Broken into a perfect square, it framed a milk-white face gazing demurely toward the empty space that had once held a painted tea table under the hovering tree.

It was then I remembered that Miss Lee had given me the plate for my birthday.

In 1942, when Roosevelt signed Executive Order 9066, my quasi-romantic ardor for the war received a setback.

Heart Mountain, in the range of the dusty hills between Grass Creek and Cody, was selected as one of the out-of-the-way sites to house West Coast Japanese Americans so they wouldn't cause trouble. They couldn't do much else either, and when my family toured the facility before it opened, I was appalled by the scabby, unpainted barracks—not insulated for the Wyoming winter—and the watch towers along the barbed-wire fence that loomed twelve feet high. Dust motes hung thick as burlap in the empty rooms, and wind flung constant dirt up through floorboards and under the ill-fitting barrack doors, so that after the camp was occupied, no matter what time of day we passed, I saw the distant housewives sweeping.

In the Thermopolis theater during newsreels, my mother applauded with the rest of the audience the staring-eyed enemy dead, and she called the Heart Mountain residents "Japs." But even she said when she glanced around the camp, "In California they can grow anything. But look at the dry gray soil they have to work with here."

Surprisingly—and possibly because nothing in the arid countryside could be harmed—able-bodied Japanese were allowed to work the sugar beet fields and were occasionally bused to Cody. So I often saw khaki buses carrying internees to town. But I also saw the WHITE ONLY signs that sprang up like dandelions in Cody so that no Japanese American could lounge by the statue of Buffalo Bill, drink a soda or eat a hamburger in the diner, or shop for a plaid shirt in the one dry-goods store.

Another event shaped my view of World War II—
and of war in general—when long before the rest of the
nation discovered the Holocaust and Hitler's Final Solution,
our tiny Wyoming elementary school learned about Third
Reich death camps.

I still have no idea how a film documenting the concentration camps could have gotten into the canister
labeled "Tooth Care" for which the school projector had
been set up, but amid the odor of lunch apples and cottonwood blazing in the stove, we sat in shocked silence
while the German cameraman panned black silhouettes of
the hanged, piles of naked bodies being shoved by bulldoz-
ers into long trenches, and heaps of clothes left beside the
doors to concrete buildings that an English voice-over said
were fake showers. "The people in line receive a bar of soap
to lull their suspicions, but once the doors are locked, poi-
son gas rather than water sprays from the shower heads."

We saw shots of lampshades and books held by grinning
Nazis while the narrator explained that the lampshades and
book covers had been made from human skin. The camera
swung past ovens, six feet long, with slots to strain out
human grease that could be used for nitroglycerine, and
the rakelike implements, also held by posing soldiers, that
pushed aside the unconsumed, charred bones. And then the
film lingered on the black billowing smoke from thousands
of incinerated human beings.

After the reels stopped, and the blinds had been raised
to daylight again, I never discussed with anyone what we'd
seen.

But the images haunted me in the night, and I saw over
and over the mound of eyeglasses that resembled the gold-
rimmed ones I wore.

During the war, my angry grandmother and my affectionate grandfather essentially disappeared from my life.

One afternoon, when I came home from school, my mother, in the kitchen making her favorite apple pie recipe, looked up and said that Ed had had a heart attack. "He just leaned over at breakfast and died." She concentrated on the crust edge she was crimping with a fork against the pie tin. "That's actually a good way to go."

I knew her offhand recital was meant to soften the death, to emphasize the painless ease of it, but somehow Ed's dying at the breakfast table—fried egg congealing on the plate, toast slipping from dead greasy fingers, gray hair on the oilcloth beside cooling coffee—was ludicrous and a little horrible, and I preferred to freeze-frame him as I'd seen him the previous Thursday, cupping his ear toward the radio with one hand, balancing the pipe toward his yellow teeth with the other. I fixed that image in my mind to remain unchanged, and when Ellen held his funeral in Thermopolis three days later, I didn't go up to view the body.

Ellen seemed to lose interest in the store without Ed to insult or command, and she left the tired bolts of calico stacked against the wall, the cans of Spam and peas on the store shelves, the antique silver bookends on the table, and the pin cushion doll on the dresser in the rooms behind the store when she abruptly sold out and bought a motel on some little-traveled highway near Kerrville, Texas.

She visited twice and bought Mike a piano because he was musical, but after she married for the fourth time, with her anger intact, she stopped coming to see us.

When anyone asks where I'm from, I say I was born in Wyoming but that I grew up in Texas, because by the time the war ended, my father had been promoted to the Texas branch of Standard Oil in Houston.

In our little oil camp, I'd spent my childhood weekends being leader of a troop of little boys tramping over the hills, but during the week, around the girls in older grades, I didn't fit in. I didn't have the same sashed cotton dresses or the same brown oxfords, and I'd had to accept that because my father was the boss and my family the aristocrats of the town, I'd naturally be treated differently—even by the teachers, who approved every sentence I wrote, every picture I colored.

I couldn't do anything about being the boss's daughter in Grass Creek, but my father had been transferred to Texas, and he was going to be in an office and not in charge of everyone else's father. So I told myself things in school would be different.

On his way to Houston, my father trained at the main office in Tulsa, and Mike and I went for a year to Wilson Junior High. Although I assured myself I didn't have close friends because I hadn't gone to elementary with anyone else in the school, I also knew it was fatal to wear glasses and make good grades.

Since I did the assignments—basically because I didn't know it was an option not to do them—there wasn't much I could do about the good grades, and since my parents couldn't have afforded contacts even if they'd heard of such a thing, there was nothing I could do about the glasses.

But we were going to Texas, and once in Texas, I'd fit in better.

When we arrived in Houston, for the first time I saw on Main Street children whose skin was actually darker than mine.

In Wyoming, Native Americans had stayed on their reservations except for rare trips to the Thermopolis thermal pool, interned Japanese Americans had scattered from Heart Mountain the minute the barbed-wire gates opened, I'd never heard of a Mexican American, and as far as I knew, no African American, except possibly a Pullman porter commuting from Cheyenne to Denver, even lived in the state. So racial divisions and "racial prejudice" didn't exist—they barely even translated—in my childhood.

But suddenly in Texas, I encountered race.

Naturally the dark-skinned children and I were kept away from each other at lunch counters, movies, and school, and when I passed them on the sidewalk, I wondered what they talked about. But of course I would never have been brave enough to try to strike up a conversation. And no matter what else my mother might have said, she'd also have said that it was rude to stare at anyone else's naturally curling hair and pigmentation, so the best I could do was nudge in beside the children before Foley's Christmas windows to watch the animated decorations.

As I stared through our reflections, I knew it was heretical even to think such a thing and I'd never have said it out loud, but I thought their images much prettier than the pale dolls inside the holiday windows.

Not unexpectedly, I didn't immediately fit in with my peers at my new school, but one reason was that I still didn't have the same clothes as all the other girls.

My mother didn't want to be a writer, but she did want to be a raconteur (I suspected she'd married to be well taken care of, but I also knew that marriage—and children—gave her a captive audience.), and she wanted to create exotic clothes—the kind of movie costumes invented by Edith Head. I'd always been thin, so she used to design and make my clothes, much as if she were dressing a paper doll, and since one of her favorite film models was black singer Lena Horne, my dresses often had elaborate skirts and petticoats with graduated layers from magenta to scarlet to lavender-pink as if I were about to star in a musical extravaganza.

When we got to Texas, I had to decide whether to demand that she let me dress like the other girls in matching sweater sets, a strand of pearls, and penny loafers, or whether I'd continue wearing her creations. Of course, even as I fielded the thought, I knew I'd no more hurt her feelings over clothes than I'd have picked—or crushed—either parent in that sinking ship scenario.

So I sighed and wore the costumes.

Every year when she grabbed the annual and saw that I hadn't been voted the best-dressed girl in my class, her face fell.

But I didn't know how to explain that the "best-dressed" honor always went to some girl in a conventional apricot sweater set, a strand of pearls, and penny loafers.

When we got to Texas, my mother would have loved a brick mansion in Houston's elegant River Oaks, but my father's salary could never swing that, so they bought a little clapboard house, surrounded by a chain-link fence, in South Houston.

South Houston should have been a Houston suburb, but it was actually a tiny scruffy town whose August streets exposed dry clods just like those in Wyoming. Mike and I still rode a bus to school—this one in nearby Pasadena—and the one grocery store was as understocked as my grandmother's had been.

For the first time, however, we had neighbors who didn't work for Standard Oil, and the burly Texan next door hadn't been in a vital industry, so he'd joined the army. One afternoon I overheard him telling my father about his part in the invasion of Italy. He'd been the first American to enter a bombed-out Italian village everyone thought had been abandoned by the Nazis, but as he rounded a corner, he came face to face with a young German soldier. They stared at each other in shock before they both smiled in the same moment of chagrin and common fright. Then he shot the kid between the eyes.

Not long after I heard that story, my English teacher asked the class to write a one-sentence memory of childhood that began "Childhood is...."

My classmates read out cheerful sentences: "Childhood is running through a field of daisies with a yellow balloon" and "Childhood is not having to worry about where we're going." When the teacher called on me, I knew mine was out of step, and I hesitated. But the class waited, and I finally had to read mine. "Childhood is really knowing why our next-door neighbor hanged himself."

My mother disliked the chain-link fence nearly as much as she did living in South Houston.

I, too, hated the fence, as well as walking to the bus, and every weekday morning, I hoped the bus would arrive at school in time for me to go to the rest room and wash off my shoes—coated with dust on dry days or mud in rainy seasons—so I'd look like a town kid. But I could forgive South Houston almost anything because it had both a theater and a library.

The movie theater sat on a side street off the highway to Galveston and played Saturday double features children could see for a nickel. We could even sit through the two features twice. The manager who put up the marquee signs couldn't spell any better than I could, and although he listed a Tarzan picture as *Tarzan's Dessert Furry*, it contained the same male adventure as the Thermopolis movies.

My mother belonged to the Book-of-the-Month Club by then, and we had bookcases stocked with such novels as *Remembrance of Things Past* and *The Grapes of Wrath*. But South Houston also had a one-room lending library, and I got a Social Security card so I could stack books after school for ten cents an hour. I'd have skipped the children's books if there'd been any, but since there weren't, I read every tattered adult volume. I started in the left corner of the room and read all the donated books on all the shelves, without interference from the librarian. I read authors no one ever heard of—as well as Grace Livingston Hill and Frank Yerby—and nearly everything I read was so bad that I concluded the only thing an author had to do to publish a novel was to finish writing it.

I wasn't ready to complete a novel, but at thirteen I thought I could manage a short story.

I'd learned by then that stories had to be typed before they could be sent to a magazine to be published and read by other people, so that first summer in South Houston, my father brought home an office typewriter so I could teach myself to type.

By August, I typed well enough on the awkward, upright Underwood to struggle through an entire manuscript, and I was ready to submit my first story. I selected *Liberty Magazine*, which took fiction and which my parents subscribed to.

My short piece, entitled "Suddenly," had framed itself as a love story. And naturally it featured a male protagonist.

I'd realized manuscripts had to be typed, but I didn't know that the author should add a self-addressed, stamped envelope, so when I mailed the story off, I left that one item out of the package.

The editor at *Liberty* who got my story must have been a really good guy—who may have perceived that I was an impossibly optimistic teenager—since not only did I get the story back but I also got a kind, handwritten rejection letter along with it.

I didn't know how rare that was, and although I did know that writers had to be persistent, I never sent the story again. It may have been that since the South Houston library lacked funds for magazine subscriptions and that other than *Liberty* my parents subscribed to *Time* and *Life*, which didn't take stories, I'd run out of places to submit.

I no longer "read" my stories to people. But I kept writing and typing them, and within a couple of years, I, like my father, had a liquor box stuffed with finished manuscripts.

Since my grandmother and mother presumably came from Texas, they probably had Southern accents, but my ear hadn't become attuned to what might befit a belle and what might not, and I wasn't really aware of how much Bea wanted to sound like Vivian Leigh playing Scarlet O'Hara until we ended up in South Houston. Then her drawl thickened enough to be unmistakably Texan.

She began lifting her chin and opening her eyelids wider than she had on the high plains (a practice that made her eyes larger and supposedly helped stymie the Texas sun wrinkles gathering on her forehead), she occasionally used a racial slur I knew she'd heard at her bridge evenings, and for some reason she decided that uttering an occasional and flirtatious "shit" when she lost a trick made her sound daring and even more Southern.

For Christmas, she bought my father a silver belt buckle centered with a long-horned, bas-relief steer ("Since you're a Taurus," she added, as if that would disguise her real intention of giving him a Texas look.), and she lavished praise on men she passed on Fannin Street who wore embossed leather cowboy boots. She smiled carmine lips and hinted that the heels on the boots would give my father the added height he needed for his greased-down hair to be level with her pompadour.

Her urging for a cowboy style was the one time I saw him resist, however, and no matter how much she bragged on the gray alligator boots in Foley's men's department, my father refused to try them on. As he later said to me, "I've already spent too much time being lower class. I'm not going to buy a pickup truck either."

I think my father always feared that his lower-class background might be exposed, so he stayed constantly on guard. He never wore anything but lace-up leather oxfords, dark suits, white starched shirts, and somber ties to his office in the Standard Oil Building, and even when he went out to weed his rose bushes that bordered the chain-link fence, he kept on the dress shoes, suit slacks, and white shirts, with the sleeves rolled up to his elbows. He never owned tennis shoes, casual khakis, or a bright yellow T-shirt.

Beyond his protective clothing, however, and possibly to add another layer to obfuscate his heritage, whenever he bought a new car, he confined himself to the acceptable middle-class brands that came in acceptable silver or black. He carried only hundred-dollar bills whenever he could, and he never went to a dinner party without taking the hostess flowers or a box of candy.

He read *Time* and *Life* from cover to cover so he'd be informed, and when he spoke—which of course wasn't often around my mother—he always selected the Latinate form of a word over its Anglo-Saxon equivalent. He never used *oily* when *oleaginous* would do, and he never said *think* if he could substitute *cogitate*. He read Shakespeare and the English writer Jeffery Farnol for their poetic language, and he read the dictionary for pleasure. Since it would have been difficult for Mike or Honey or me not to absorb his interest in words, all three of us ended up with great vocabularies.

I knew all the time, of course, that I'd use the words in my own stories.

One afternoon my father came home from work and stopped in the dining room. He stood there, looked down at my watercolor sketch of the orange dog flopped out asleep on the rug, and after a moment said, "It's not possible for someone to be great in two different fields. I think you need to decide which you want to do, write or paint."

Most weekends, I alternated days sitting at the dining room table penciling rough drafts of stories or completing watercolors, and I wasn't certain why he thought someone couldn't do both.

But since he silently debated things like that more than I did, and since he was the most intelligent, the most rational man I knew, I nodded. "If you think so."

"You write more than you paint, so you probably should go with that."

If being successful depended on perseverance, I had enough to fill half a dozen more cardboard boxes with manuscripts. So I nodded again.

I continued to paint, I took the Galveston-to-Houston bus once a week to an art course at the museum, and in high school I convinced the assistant principal to let me substitute drawing class for study hall, but I never considered painting anything but a hobby. I'd occasionally show a watercolor to a friend, mention my father's caution, and occasionally someone would say, "Are you sure you didn't make the wrong choice?"

But after that dining room moment, I knew I wouldn't consider art an option.

I knew I'd write instead.

I suppose I'd accepted for a long time, without articulating it, that my father drank too much.

When he came home from his seventeenth-floor office in the Standard Oil Building in his white shirt, tie, dark suit, and lace-up oxfords, he always had at least two tumblers of Old Granddad with a splash of tap water before dinner and at least two more bourbons and water in the den afterward. He didn't need to *sound* sober since my mother did all the talking, and he could gaze at her and nod at the right pauses in her stories.

My mother drank with him, but all of us knew her glass held weak tea, which she pretended was straight bourbon on the rocks—the way she pretended at parties so people would smile and excuse her for being high if she laughed and flirted too much—so he was essentially drinking alone. Since my father didn't talk unless he'd thought over a problem and could offer a solution, she could ignore that his green eyes turned glassy sometime during the evening, and she never mentioned that he might have drunk too much unless he intended to drive.

But at the end of the evening, he always staggered and fell against the table, knocking over the salt shaker and sluicing water from the bowl with the magnolia blossom, on his way through the kitchen.

None of us mentioned that either, because drinking was what professional people—particularly men, and especially those of Irish ancestry—did to blur the fact that all the other men on the seventeenth floor were college graduates.

I looked more like my father than my mother, and although my eyes were brown rather than green, I did have his almost nonexistent lips, his nearly black hair, and his swarthy ("black") Irish olive skin. We were both thin (He'd once put on weight—which he said meant he was successful—but he lost it again after my mother, watching him pat his enlarged stomach, said, "I don't find fat men sexy."), and I suppose we were both small even though I thought for years that I'd grown to his height.

I also strove to emulate his calm personality. His studied tranquility may have been as much a mask as his language and clothes, but to me, he didn't seem to need to perform the way my mother did, and I, too, wanted to be able to sit still and listen and not have to be center stage. I tried to be someone who could reason things out and understand, and while I accepted Fate and I recognized that I had his genes as well as those of my obese grandmother, Nella May, I told myself I could limit what I ate and what I drank.

Alcohol had always been a part of our family life, and even as a little girl, I remember drinking bourbon-spiked eggnog from Ellen's purple Tom and Jerry cups. Mike and I were allowed wine on holidays, and I'm sure if either of us had asked, my father would have fixed us an evening drink so he'd have company.

But as I watched my intelligent father slur his hard-learned words, stumble and crash into the bookcase, I knew that while I couldn't pretend with iced tea, I could learn to handle what I did drink.

And I'd make sure never to drink alone.

My mother hadn't wanted the inconvenience of a third child ("One boy and one girl make a perfect boxed set."), and when my little sister, Honey, was born, her resentment was palpable. So before long I became more or less a surrogate nanny.

I always thought Honey a beautiful little girl, and whenever I took her on the bus into Houston, I was always gratified by the fact that women would stop me on the sidewalk outside Foley's and comment on what a pretty child I had with me. By fourteen, I'd observed that women complimented other people's children in order to please the mothers, and since I obviously wasn't Honey's mother, their admiration served to strengthen my faith in her beauty.

I also thought she was a really smart little kid who'd be able to do anything she wanted. Although she didn't take after me and she admired magic over gravity, I knew she should be a scientist of some kind.

One time during a spring ball season, my friend Allene and I took Honey shopping, and she stared happily into the plate-glass window full of glittering prom gowns. When we were ready to move on, Allene said, "Which did you like best?"

Honey glanced up. "What?"

"Did you like the sequined or the satin dresses better?"

"Oh, those." She shrugged her bony shoulders. "Look here at this hole in the window." Her little finger touched a tiny circle in the glass. "They had too much oxygen in the mix and the glass imploded and made these bubbles."

I occasionally took Honey with me to Saturday movies. I had accepted that she was too small to sit through a double feature twice, and whenever I walked her along the dirt street to the theater, I steeled myself to leave after one viewing.

She was little enough to get in free, so I'd spend her nickel on Jordan almonds or slimy Jujubes, and she always sat quietly through the coming attractions, the serial, and the opening feature while she sucked happily on whatever candy I picked out for her. Even though I personally liked newsreels, I realized whenever I had Honey with me that her licorice whips might not last through the news, too, and it was just as well the manager cut the Pathé reels from his children's afternoons.

We were generally joined by some South Houston boy who wanted to impress me, and I particularly remember the afternoon John Allen sat with us and blew—throughout the short subjects—increasingly larger, and more fragile, pink bubble gum globes. Just before the movie started, however (The cowboy film usually came on before the romantic comedy.), John Allen leaned over too far to show me his bubble, and the gum got caught in Honey's hair.

John Allen and I tried to pick it out, but the entangled pink gum and baby-fine hair were too much for us, and Honey got so distressed that I finally had to walk her home.

I hadn't even made it to Roy Rogers, and I was so angry with John Allen that no matter how vehemently he apologized, I refused to have anything to do with him for two weeks.

"It's hard to write fiction for a living. You need an occupation to fall back on."

My father had guided the decision, but he'd obviously been reconsidering it (He'd have said "ruminating on it."), and I wondered if he'd tried selling fiction while amassing that box of manuscripts and reputedly going to barber school. But that particular night he'd already started on his third bourbon and branch, so I didn't ask.

"No woman should be dependent on a husband." He spoke carefully, enunciating each word, with deliberate attention to the vowels, the way he did after too many drinks. "If she made a mistake in the marriage, she needs to be able to throw the son of a bitch out. No woman should give up anything she wants to do just to be a wife."

My mother was playing bridge that evening, and I doubted he'd have murmured an opinion so opposed to hers if she'd been home. He could have been thinking about what she herself might have sacrificed to be provided for— or possibly what he'd given up to take care of her—but I didn't ask that either.

"As long as you have a profession and can support yourself, you can stay single or you can bring home a gorilla if you want to."

It was a given that all of us would go to college, so I said, "I'm just trying to decide whether to major in English or history or languages."

He drained his glass and stood up unsteadily to get a refill. "Why not major in all three? Then you can choose what you want to teach."

I heard the echo of my mother insisting that grade school teaching was permissible woman's work, and I said, "I'll teach in college of course."

45

Pasadena High School, one of the best industrial—
and most segregated—high schools in Texas, sat across the
channel from a paper mill, and anyone who graduated or
dropped out in tenth grade could get a job. So few students
took college-track classes.

There were ten of us in Miss Mayfield's Latin class,
twelve in her American literature, and when she decided
to introduce her "special students" to the finer things, she
selected a few college-bound scholars to take in a Houston
dinner and movie. She chose a Chinese restaurant—for
its cultural component—before we went to Lowe's for
Olivier's *Hamlet*. As she taught us how to hold chopsticks, I
didn't have the heart to tell her that my mother had already
instructed Mike and me in their use.

I don't know if Bill, Dee, and Martha had also learned
to wield chopsticks at home, but when Miss Mayfield said
over fortune cookies, "You all must learn to play bridge. It's
a genteel game you'll need to know as college graduates,"
none of us told her we four already played bridge every
weekend.

She pointedly valued "special" students above the run-
of-the-mill ones who would eventually work at the mill,
and so for our dinner and movie, she hadn't invited orange-
haired, freckled Jimmy Vinson. He was one of the brightest kids in my class, but his mother ran the liquor store on
Galveston Highway where airmen training at Ellington
Field stopped to buy beer, so Miss Mayfield hadn't considered him.

He lived with his mother in a cramped apartment next
to the store, and since she often invited customers over for
a drink on the house, I knew that both he and his mother
would have appreciated it if he could have had a night out
with Miss Mayfield.

Dee, Bill, Martha, and I played bridge or picnicked on the sand of Galveston Beach, but the three of them were a school year behind me, so I spent class time with Jimmy. He told me almost as soon as he sat down beside me in trigonometry that he was gay. "I knew when I was five and fell in love with my brother's best friend."

That older brother was off at Texas A&M, so their mother bought Jimmy a car—which none of us whose mothers didn't run liquor stores could afford—to get him out of her way. I don't think he had any other friends, and he dropped by my house, generally after 10:00 p.m., whenever his mother had company.

Since he wrote, too, he often read me his stories. I'd learned by then that other writers preferred to read me their stories rather than listen to mine, and I don't remember bringing out any manuscript from my cardboard boxes for Jimmy. I do remember that most of his stories contained carrot-haired protagonists and some reference to homosexuality, and I also remember my father saying one evening as Jimmy stopped his car out front, "Don't even imagine you can change him. It can't be done."

Jimmy had moved to the highway liquor store from a metropolitan area a couple of years earlier, and since he hadn't had to limit his reading to his mother's bookcase or to the single room of the South Houston library, he knew more about literature than I did. So the first time I encountered Joyce's *Ulysses* was when Jimmy sat on my mother's green silk Queen Anne couch and read aloud the entire Molly Bloom section—which must have taken him until two or three in the morning. I knew it had to be an important book, but somehow in his voice it sounded freckled and a trifle dull.

In the '30s and '40s my mother—maybe every American mother—yearned to have a little curly-headed moppet like Shirley Temple for a daughter, and at least two or three times a year, she packed me off to a beauty parlor for a permanent. My first time at the Thermopolis beauty salon, I must have been four, and since in those years a full set of curls came only from a machine whose electric clamps crisped bales of hair into the wiry ringlets Shirley wore, I was hooked up to rollers and the machine's thick black wires. I was too small to sit in the chair while the electric current cooked my straight, too-fine strands, and I felt as if hours passed before a beautician noticed the tears running down my cheeks and realized I was essentially hanging from the machine by my hair.

By the time I got to high school, the home permanent kit had come on the market, and my mother could create those lush curls for me herself.

I loved the curly hair I saw on the black kids in Houston, but I despised my own curls that turned limp and dangled to the top of my clear plastic glasses by noon. So one Saturday while my mother was out shopping, I persuaded my father (who still owned the scissors from that course in barbering he said he took) to give me a boy cut.

When my mother got home, I had a cropped wing of bangs across my forehead and beautifully clipped featherings an inch long over the rest of my head. Since that same afternoon I'd also meticulously painted the clear plastic frames of my glasses, using a bottle of her scarlet fingernail polish, I was a new person.

But my mother wept for three days for my curls and didn't speak to my father for a week.

I envied my classmates who came back from Christmas break brandishing a dollar bill awarded for the A on their semester report card. Over the holidays, I'd taken a job in the toy department of Sears to be able to buy presents, and even fifty cents for each A would have made my bargain hunting easier. Of course I probably would have appreciated nearly as much as the cash any notice from my parents that *all* the grades on my card were As. But academic achievement was something they both considered standard for us, and my mother often shrugged and said, "Why would anyone carry a pint in a gallon jug?" Neither my mother nor my father made anything of—or even acknowledged—the two gold medals I collected at baccalaureate evenings for being the top student in the sophomore class and in the junior class, or the two gold medallions that confirmed me the best all-around Pasadena High School graduate and valedictorian of the senior class.

After we all got out of college, neither of them ever commented on my Phi Beta Kappa key or seemed to think Mike's, Honey's, or my Ph.D. anything out of the ordinary. And in fact, once when I introduced my mother to Bob Lewis, and he said, "That's *Dr.* Lewis. I have a Ph.D.," my mother gave him her arch glance and said without missing a beat, "Doesn't everybody?"

I don't recall my father being impressed by any of my accomplishments through the blur that was high school, but my mother enjoyed the fact that I usually had a date for the prom ("It doesn't matter if this one is good-looking or smart; go out with him so other boys will notice you."), and she could design a new costume for me to exhibit.

I somehow suspected all the time that I had to leave Danny in my childhood. I wasn't sure he'd learned to read from the back row in our classroom or that he'd even reached eighth grade, and I knew I had to make it as a writer—with an education and without him. But my mother had kept one friend in Grass Creek, and through her, I heard that Danny had become a roustabout. Once the friend sent a group picture taken at a picnic that included Danny, and I saw that he was as handsome as he'd been as a child.

I don't think my mother could be impressed by heroism, and she further dismissed Danny because she considered him illegitimate. From the rules of genetics she'd deduced that two blue-eyed parents couldn't produce a brown-eyed child, and since the Delaneys both had pale, wormy complexions and faded-blue-jean eyes, together they couldn't have spawned Danny with his almost Indian-dark skin and large eyes of deep brown.

My mother did recognize good-looking when she saw it, however, so when my father was sent from the Houston office to take an inventory of oilfield equipment in the Grass Creek area, my mother went along, carrying my senior class photo to give to Danny. As she tucked the picture in her bag, I guessed she wanted to bask in his dark-eyed attention while she told him—albeit briefly—about me.

But when she returned from Wyoming, she didn't offer any details about the trip except to say that she'd handed the picture to Danny. Since I didn't want to hear how kind and noticing he was or that he was about to marry some pretty blond cheerleader, I never pressed her to elaborate on her meeting with him.

Pasadena High reluctantly bowed to good economic times and arranged a weeklong journey across Texas for a senior class trip. The school district wasn't sophisticated enough to give the nod to a coed trip, so they set up a trip for the girls—the boys went a month later—and in orange buses we barreled down the highway toward El Paso.

Like the land of my childhood, West Texas lay open, vast, and straightforward. In daylight, the sun beamed down with the unrelenting glare of a monstrous magnifying glass—so hot and focused that within five minutes one of my pale friends, Gracie, cooked shrimp pink. At night, the sky, scrubbed clean of dust, showed uncannily brilliant stars hanging in the midnight-blue darkness like stationary plane lights, and we sat on sleeping bags, clasping our knees and watching for a while before we decided they were actually stars.

When we reached El Paso and crossed the bridge into Mexico, we entered not only another country but another world, this one filled with chili-infused air, loud Spanish, and overcrowded shops hung with cheap cotton blouses embroidered with red and yellow poppies or draped with festoons of hammered silver necklaces.

Gracie clutched my arm as we skirted the beggars sheltering sleeping babies in their grimy shawls, she gazed with dismay at the trays of sliced pineapple and at the dark-eyed vendors holding the fruit disks out to us and shouting, *"Un peso, niñas,"* and she cringed the entire length of Juarez Avenue. I let her hang onto me, but I was thrilled to be purchasing a sterling bracelet for me and a turquoise ring for Honey in such boisterous and vibrating foreignness where one only had to cross a bridge to be submerged in utterly new stories.

During our senior year, the school board mandated a battery of standardized tests—from IQ to achievement to personality—and that spring our class spent hours in the cafeteria's 100° April humidity filling in damp circles on damp exam pages. As perspiration dripped off my forehead, I knew Rock Smith lost at least a dozen IQ points when halfway through the timed test he handed me his clean handkerchief to wipe streams of sweat from the lenses of my crimson-framed glasses.

It was the personality test, however, that hardened my belief in the utter worthlessness of all standardized exams.

I had been elected class secretary—the one female position among the four class offices—because I'd managed the election. On the El Paso trip, as we sat around a campfire, I'd suggested that since girls on the unpopular bus outnumbered girls on the popular bus, we should nominate one of our own and elect her by superior numbers. Even as I said it, I knew I'd be the logical choice. So when the personality test asked "Do people like you?" and offered the standard answers of "Yes," "No," or "I don't know," I had to decide on the basis that I'd manipulated the girls into choosing, and hence "liking," me.

The only possible answer was "I don't know."

Jimmy struggled with the questions because he knew America's views on homosexuality, but Don Brady blithely chose all "Yes" on one page, all "No" on the next.

The three of us made a score of 5 out of 100, and we had to repeat the test.

By then we knew that the shocked teachers would make us take it until we gave the *right* answers, so surprisingly, on the very next try, we each scored a 95.

As valedictorian of the senior class, I received one hundred dollars from the Pasadena Rotary Club, and I used the money to travel to New York City, where all famous American authors lived and wrote, and where I'd live and write when I got out of school. I had to return to Houston for college, but I told myself I'd go east as soon as I got a B.A.

With the Rotary Club check, I bought a round-trip bus ticket, booked hotels in New Orleans, Washington, New York, and Chicago, and had enough left for a chopped liver sandwich every noon and a balcony seat for Mary Martin's *Peter Pan*.

On the leg of the journey from New Orleans to Washington, I met an older man—possibly all of twenty-one—with whom I necked most of the way to D.C. He lived in New York, in an apartment in the Bronx, and as he wrote his phone number in my notebook and changed buses, he said, "Call me from the Port Authority."

Two days later, the Greyhound bus cruised along the highway from Washington, and I debated whether or not to give him a call and go to the Bronx. He was very good-looking and very romantic, but he was old. And adult New York men might be more insistent than the Pasadena boys I knew.

I stared out the bus window into the sunlight and wished I could talk to my father with his rational approach. I could mull over the dilemma with him and decide.

Abruptly a billboard loomed at the side of the road. It advertised some brand of insurance and showed a highway accident in which a bleeding family limped away from a mangled car. The huge caption blazed in red letters, WHY TAKE CHANCES?

I knew at once that if Fate sent such unmistakable messages, I had to listen.

The minute I got off the bus in the Port Authority and climbed the marble staircase to the sidewalk littered with cigarette butts, I knew this city was where I did indeed belong. A rain had recently passed through, and as I inhaled the odor of wet pavement and sodden newspaper in the gutter, I told myself that when I graduated from college, New York City—containing all those stoops Cagney died on—was my destiny.

I found the McAlpine Hotel with my reserved room, called the handsome older man in the Bronx to say that I couldn't come by after all, and when I emerged from the lobby into the street again, I fell instantly in love with the evening glow of the Empire State Building and the crowd. Despite the myths I'd heard about brusque New Yorkers, whenever I stopped to consult my map, someone always paused to offer directions.

I also fell in love with the theater, and I easily ignored the wire as Mary Martin in her Peter Pan suit whirled above the audience. But since she whirled a long time, night had fallen by the time the play ended and I started down Broadway toward my hotel.

Three men, probably young though it was too dark to tell, came toward me on the sidewalk. As they passed me, they separated and grabbed my arms above the elbows.

Just then, a cab pulled over to the curb, and the driver leaned toward the passenger window. "The boys giving you trouble, miss?"

The men were startled enough to relax their grip, and before they recovered, I pulled my arms free and raced off. I breathlessly reached the lobby and assured myself that when I came to New York to live, I'd learn what to avoid. It couldn't be any harder than learning to tell which tumbleweed on the prairie sheltered a coiled rattler.

In 1950 the pink brick buildings of Rice University (then called "Rice Institute" as if agronomists sat at lab tables perfecting porcelain white rice grains) enclosed each side of a manicured quadrangle just off Houston's South Main. Done in ornate faux Mediterranean with carved stone owls (the Rice mascot) on columns and cornices, the rose brick facades made a stunning backdrop for floodlit performances of *Macbeth* and appeared in daylight to belong to some exquisitely liberal and humanistic college.

But when I entered Rice, the school barely offered a liberal education. It eschewed Greek, art, drama, and music and considered even geology, archaeology—and literature written after 1900—frivolous. The dim interiors of the pink buildings housed a few classrooms but a great many chemistry, biology, and engineering labs.

A bronze statue of the founder, William Marsh Rice, seated high on a pedestal in the square, was occasionally enameled vivid orange by Texas University students before games or hoisted and revolved 180 degrees by bright Rice engineers before finals. The wealthy Texan, William Rice, supposedly murdered by his butler trying—without success—to stop the nonsense of bequeathing money to a college, had had an ideal of an all-white, tuition-free space for four hundred top students. The students, mostly valedictorians and salutatorians from white high schools in Texas (fewer than two hundred of whom ever lasted four years), spent a grand total of a twenty-five-dollar library fee each year.

So when my father said, "Make good grades and go to Rice or find a job and pay your way through some other college," Mike, Honey, and I all got Rice diplomas.

My freshman English class was taught by a new graduate student, a twenty-six-year-old bomber pilot from World War II by the name of James Dickey, who'd come to Rice to work on a Ph.D. The class was held in a biology lab, and Dickey often vaulted onto the lab table and strode back and forth, his saddle shoes and argyle socks at eye level, while he pontificated on poetry and handed back our red-inked freshman themes.

"Miss Moore," he leveled at me one morning. "You're a damned good writer, but goddamn, have you read some awful stuff. Drop by my office and bring your themes."

When I got to his glass-windowed carrel in the library basement, *he* talked—a little about making every word count, but mostly about sex. ("You have a beautiful mouth. Anybody ever told you that? It's probably the most beautiful mouth I ever saw." or "Have you ever thought it'd be interesting to have sex while your hands were tied? Or chained to a wall?") He often lamented—naïvely, I thought—that we met in the library rather than in a darkened lounge. "If I go out with Maxine, she brings up insurance or dental bills. I want to hold someone's hand and discuss literature and writing." And once he said, "Come to my apartment for tea on Sunday. Do you like beer?"

I asked my friend Allene, also in Dickey's English 100, to come along, and we arrived at his apartment in heels and white gloves to be met by a bare-chested, bare-footed Jim clad only in gym shorts. "Come on in."

I didn't glance at Allene to gauge her reaction, but I swallowed hard, and my own glove didn't stop shaking until we stepped into the apartment and saw Jim's wife, Maxine, coming down the hall carrying a tray with a tea set and cups.

Rice had opened in 1912 as a coed college, but with its concentration on the sciences, male students in 1950 still outnumbered the females eight to one. Given that ratio, it seemed only natural for me to go to every prom and football game. On weekends, I'd have a lunch date, a date for the matinee at the Alley Theatre, and yet another for dinner. One Saturday and Sunday I sat through *A Place in the Sun* twice because both young men had counted on seeing it with me.

When a classmate of Mike's asked why I was so popular, I know he hoped to hear that I slept with everyone, but Mike said, "Because she's ugly. Pretty girls scare guys, but Pat never scares anyone."

I not only didn't scare guys, I made them comfortable. I'd learned by then that if a female posed questions and listened to the answers, any male would talk and talk and come bounding back. So I asked, listened, and added follow-ups. Since I also let the novice scientists hold my hand and kiss me good night at the door, I was a godsend to the high-grade-point Rice undergraduates whom girls had spurned in high school.

And by the end of my freshman year, I could recognize—in seconds—which young men would be worthless as dates or characters.

One architecture major whose name I don't recall took me to a new Houston restaurant, and when the waiter brought the basket of dinner rolls, I noticed that the chef had scorched all but one of them. I couldn't miss the fact that the young architect, while answering one of my queries, pawed through the basket to take out the single unburnt roll. I was always busy whenever he called again.

The Korean War had started the summer before my freshman year, and since Dickey had joined the reserves after World War II, he spent only the first semester at Rice before he was called back to air force duty. Allene and I took up a collection from the class and bought him a silver watch fob with his initials (for James Lafayette Dickey III—though I think we left off the III) engraved on a very masculine sterling rectangle.

He was gone for two years before he reappeared on the Rice campus.

Our talks in his office resumed, but now that I was a junior, I talked, too, when we discussed writing and he read me parts of his novel—which wasn't *Deliverance* but a roman à clef full of male angst and obvious poetic images. ("Did you notice that yellow bowl of flowers I put in? Yellow is brittle, and I want this to be a flinty scene.") He now lamented that he couldn't have an affair with a student ("It would ruin my career. I'd never teach again."), while he regaled me with his heroic experiences of being shot down in the Pacific and of flying bombing missions over Korea. He recommended writers like Bowles and Proust and urged me to focus on French literature because he'd read everything in English worth reading, and I didn't need to waste my time plowing through the canon of British literature.

Unfortunately, he also introduced me to the literary concept of "It's who you know in publishing" the day I heard I got a story accepted in the Rice publication, *Soundings*. I rushed into his office to tell him my great news.

He nodded. "I'm the faculty sponsor. I made sure your story got a good reading."

I didn't snarl, "Thanks a lot," but I wanted to.

Rice at the time offered one creative writing class.

My high school buddy, Jimmy Vinson, who'd started Rice with me, took all the English classes I did, so we both signed up for creative writing, taught by George Williams, who had a book on writing and a novel, *The Blind Bull*. I don't know if Jimmy read both books before he took the course, but I did and decided I could learn something from Williams even though he didn't have a Ph.D. and was disdained by the department elite.

We spent class time reading and discussing theory, which I found fascinating and which Jimmy loathed. Sharing manuscripts was relegated to one evening a week at Williams's house near the Rice campus. Jimmy and I always went together since he had the car. I remember those evenings with affection, but I can recall only one story from the entire year, Jimmy's, whose climax had two boys kissing in a swimming pool.

Kindly, gray-haired, and gray-eyebrowed George Williams unfortunately never emphasized authenticity in fiction, and I learned to recognize only in a hazy way what distinguished a good story from a merely competent one. It would take years for me to unlearn many of the methods we labored over, and since he recommended reading daily papers for story ideas, I ultimately had to discover the importance of vision, voice, and point of view on my own.

When I returned for George's ninetieth birthday celebration at Rice, I realized I was as fond of him as ever, but I also decided that perhaps every aspiring writer should take only one creative writing course to learn how not to write.

After we moved to South Houston, we never had another vegetable garden, and instead my father planted Talisman roses—whose thorns left great purple blood pools under the skin on his arms—and the kind of magnolia trees that grew in yards of the wealthy. But he also monitored a great expanse of well-trimmed lawn around the magnolias, and when he decided to buy a bomb shelter, he had plenty of room for it.

One afternoon when Mike and I came home from the Rice campus, my father was sitting with a glass of bourbon at the kitchen table spread with brochures, and I could tell the bomb shelter salesman had been there.

"Did you buy one?"

He shook his head. "I told him to cancel the contract."

I looked down at the glossy photos of the various igloolike concrete structures. "I thought you wanted a bomb shelter."

"I thought so, too." He fingered the brochures and picked one up. "This shelter was the right size for the five of us to live in for a month after an atomic blast. We could store enough food and water to last until the fallout dissipated."

"And?"

He opened the brochure to the photograph of a high-powered rifle on the inside flap. "But it came with this. If I get the shelter, I'm supposed to stand at the door and shoot anyone else who tries to crowd in."

He slapped the brochure shut onto the table and picked up his tumbler. "That means all the little kids in the neighborhood."

My sophomore year at Rice I persuaded the English Department to let me sign up for an extra class, so while full-time was fifteen hours a semester, I took eighteen. That same year I also started to work in Rice's Fondren Library—for fifty cents an hour—and although the library lacked contemporary novels, the open stacks and rare books room ignited my imagination even more than movie theaters had.

My father had been right. I could work, go out three or four times a week, and major in English, history, and languages all at the same time. Classes were held six days a week, and when Mike—with whom I shared a ride to school since there were no dorms for girls—worked in his physics lab across campus on Saturdays, I got out of class and sat in the library to wait for my evening date while I read Molière's plays, every book on the Civil War, everything related to the Holocaust, everything on the Black Death.

No student could go part-time to Rice, but the university did hand out one-hundred-dollar scholarships to top full-time students, so I went home with an application.

My father looked at it. "You don't need this. Rice is free. You can make good grades even while you work at the library. In all fairness, you need to let other working students, who can't excel in class as easily, apply for that money."

I sighed.

I didn't remind him that a hundred dollars was two hundred hours of filing subject cards in the library card catalogue.

Nor did I ever tell him that one of my friends, who'd been awarded one of the scholarships, bought herself a diamond pinkie ring with the money.

The summer after my junior year, I went to Europe
with ninety Canadian soldiers.

Of course, I didn't actually go to Europe *with* them, but
we chugged across the Atlantic together on a rusted Greek
boat that labeled itself a cruise ship.

The Canadians, draftees heading for their German rota-
tion, were a last-minute addition, and just before the paint-
flaking ship sailed from the St. Lawrence, they marched
smartly up the gangplank in their khaki wool uniforms.
The Greek line apparently saw no problem jamming ninety
more bodies aboard since the Canadians were mostly working class, and the other voyagers were students on cheap
European vacations. My own three-hundred-dollar tour included the ocean liner, youth hostels offering breakfast and
lunch, and a bus—with a Dutch guide—that would careen
through France, Luxembourg, Belgium, the Netherlands,
Germany, Switzerland, and Italy carrying twenty of us.

Naturally the entire meal arrangements on the ship had
to be junked, and the first evening as I came in to dinner,
seven soldiers filled the eight places at my assigned table.
Traveling alone from Houston, I hadn't yet met anyone,
and since I didn't know the new seating plans, I joined the
young Canadians. I asked about Canada; they talked and
clamored for my exclusive attention the rest of the voyage.

Not until we disembarked at Le Havre did I meet the
other students.

As we waited on the pier for our bus, one of them asked,
"Did all ninety soldiers kiss you good-bye?"

"I didn't count."

I crossed the Pont Neuf and knew that in Paris I could *really* write.

I stood breathing in the oily scent of the Seine and ancient paper smells of the bookseller stalls as the sun sank behind the Louvre and a young Frenchman stopped beside me to offer a cigarette from a crumpled pack. I'd never learned to inhale, but I took the cigarette and he lit it with a French match that he struck on his thumbnail.

He lowered his lids, gazed seductively through the smoke, and touched one of my daisy-shaped earrings with a nicotine-stained finger. Then he asked me a question.

I'd never fooled myself about my facility for languages (I'd racked up two years of Latin, five years of French, one year of German, one of Italian, and one of Russian.), and despite my conviction that the truly educated must know multiple languages, I could tell I'd never be able to use effectively the synonyms, metaphors, and nuances of any language but English. And although I could read, write, and make As in the foreign tongues I studied, I couldn't speak anything except English.

So I had no idea what the young Frenchman had asked. And I had to content myself with shaking my head.

He stood with me while I finished the uninhaled cigarette and tossed it after his into the twilight river. Then he gave me a look of exaggerated regret and caressed the flower attached to my earlobe again before he strolled on down the sidewalk.

I watched him—along with my futile desire to be a citizen of the world—disappear into the Parisian crowd.

Conventional wisdom in the 1950s contained two rhetorical questions: "How can you think of yourself as a painter if you can't draw a straight line?" and "How could you possibly be a writer if you can't spell?" I suppose if anyone had actually asked either question, my answers would have been, "If you need to draw a straight line, get a ruler." Or "Narration, motivation, and vocabulary have nothing to do with spelling."

In fact, as much as I revered words, I spelled so badly that if Honey asked Mike whether the vowel in a word was an *a* or an *e*, he always said, "Go ask Pat. Whichever way she spells it, use the other one. She's never gotten a word right yet."

My father decided I read too fast to focus on the letters themselves and thus I couldn't visualize—or spell—words; my mother decided it was because schools had dropped phonetics; my Rice professors finally decided that perhaps "understanding" and "spelling" weren't inextricably intertwined and that I was merely brain-damaged. Which allowed them to stop subtracting points on my exams. ("You have all the answers right, but you have so many misspelled words you'd fail the test if I took off for spelling.") I was never able to explain it myself since I didn't have dyslexia (which no one had heard of anyway), and I ultimately had to accept that I just couldn't spell.

Rice had a spelling test, however, that every student had to pass before graduation, and while most freshmen sailed through it, I was still repeating it as a senior.

At last, one of my graduate student friends, Jim Young, in the Ph.D. program with Dickey, conducted the test and pronounced the words with such exaggeration ("Next word, Wool-ly.") that I finally made a 63, a score high enough to pass.

My most important hero/mentor at Rice was English professor and department head Alan Dougal McKillop, who taught Dante, Chaucer, and the English novel from the beginning. It was in his class that I read *Tom Jones* and recognized for the first time what constituted real literature. In his class I read four Thomas Hardy novels—because McKillop loved them—before I decided I couldn't stand the bleak and laborious Hardy.

Jim Dickey hated McKillop, who insisted that he earn a Ph.D. to stay at Rice, and occasionally Jim would sidle up and say, "Why don't we organize a May Day parade? Let's get back at fat ass McKillop." Jim and I still talked in his office at least once a week, or he'd stroll through the stacks where I sat reading and drop a book in my lap. "Read this." Or he'd say, "You're going to be Phi Beta Kappa, aren't you? If I can be, you can. I'll turn you over my knee if you aren't." Or he'd ask about my dates: "Is that Kantor kid you're going with rich?" "How about Henry? You interested in him?"

The last semester of my senior year, he came by and said, "You're staying here for grad school, aren't you? Have you thought about a thesis? We could do a great one if I direct it. Why don't you talk to McKillop about me being your graduate advisor."

I knew I couldn't write on Conrad—a favorite of mine, but still in the English canon—if Jim were the advisor, but I dutifully stopped Dr. McKillop one afternoon as we crossed the quadrangle together and asked if Jim could be my thesis director.

McKillop's Coke-bottle glasses glittered in the sun as he laughed.

The next year when I entered the graduate program, Jim was no longer at Rice, and Dr. McKillop appointed himself the director of my thesis on Joseph Conrad.

"That Kantor kid" Dickey had asked about was Tim Kantor, a blind date from Ellington, whose father had written the smash Academy Award–winning movie *Best Years of Our Lives*. Tim had entered the air force rather than college, but his friend in Houston was the son of actor Cecil Calloway, and when I mentioned that, Jim was duly impressed.

I'd been out with Tim a few times (listening to him talk about Hollywood and his father's books) before he called to say that his mother and father were coming to town and that he wanted them to meet me.

My mother delightedly sewed up an elegant, black, off-the-shoulder blouse and swirling black skirt for me, and Tim and I met his parents at the Hilton's Emerald Room, an unbelievably expensive and unbelievably gaudy place, sporting boulder-sized faux emeralds. I don't remember Tim's mother except that she was motherly, but I do remember MacKinlay Kantor wore brown shoes with his black suit. He looked at our table and said to the waiter, "Where's the manager? I don't think you know who I am."

The manager gave us a table next to the dance floor and two more waiters.

Once after Tim and I danced and came back to the table, his father stood up, traced his hand across my bare shoulders, and said, "Now where was it Tim found you?"

Over after-dinner coffee we talked about fiction, and MacKinlay Kantor said he was an expert on the Civil War. I'd read a lot about the Civil War myself, but I knew better than to say that to a man who thought himself an authority, so I merely plied him with questions.

Tim naturally called again. And again.

The summer before I started graduate school, I decided not to drive to Oxford, Mississippi, with Henry and Bill to meet William Faulkner.

"He's a Nobel Prize winner, Pat. Jim Dickey says he and Faulkner are good friends. He likes Dickey's poetry and he's a real author, not a Hollywood hack."

Jim had never mentioned Faulkner, so I suspected his "good friends" description was hedging a bit.

"Come on, Pat. It'll be fun."

They were both gay, and I knew it would be perfectly safe to go anywhere with them, but I'd read only two Faulkner novels, *As I Lay Dying* and *Sanctuary*, and I hadn't liked either very much. I decided I wouldn't know what to say to an author, even a Nobel Prize one, whose work I didn't respond to. So I said, "I don't think I'll go this time."

Henry and Bill sent me a postcard saying that Faulkner was a great guy even if he was a drunk, and that I'd have had a good time.

Then on the way back from Mississippi, Henry, driving Bill's little VW, hit a mule. Bill was thrown out the passenger side, his head hit a rock at the edge of the road, and he died instantly.

Bill had had a fifteen-hundred-dollar Rice teaching assistantship, and that summer Dr. McKillop offered me one.

But I carefully never asked if it had any connection to Bill's death.

Besides Jimmy, I had three other good friends in college, Allene Hopfe, my ally in Dickey's class who worked in the registrar's office and sneaked out our grades ahead of semester reports; Nancy Wright, a girl secure enough to date my friend Bill, who was a dwarf; and Bob Curl, who graduated with the top honors in our class.

I liked Bob a lot, and our last semester we dated every Saturday, spent an occasional weekend with his sister in Freeport, and sat knee to knee in philosophy. Then one day before class when he mused, "I want to marry someone pretty," I knew that let me out. So I gave up the idea of marrying him as he went off to grad school at Berkeley.

I stayed at Rice and started going with a handsome blond graduate student in biology, Jack Esslinger, whom I'd met at the Phi Beta Kappa banquet, and by the time Bob came back to Houston during the Christmas holidays and asked me to marry him, I was already involved with Jack.

I walked across campus to the biology building and went into Jack's lab.

His master's thesis, on the life cycle of the flesh-devouring *Callitroga hominivorax*, made his lab reek of rotting meat as the screw-worm larvae ate holes in the sides of guinea pigs. The little animals stood wavering in their cages while maggot tails bobbed in the wounds like slow-bouncing pearls and Jack sat in a white lab coat at a microscope counting guinea pig white cells. He waved but kept staring in the eyepiece.

"Bob just asked me to marry him. Do you want me to go back to the library and tell him I will or do you want to marry me?"

He didn't look up from the microscope. "I'll marry you."

For my birthday, I treated myself to a copy of MacKinlay Kantor's *Andersonville*.

During the few months I'd gone with Tim, he'd given me a portrait of himself in dress uniform, and when he'd transferred from Ellington for bombardier training, he'd hinted broadly that we should get together when he came back.

I stalled.

I knew I should write to him about Jack, but I didn't get around to it before his letters trickled off and then ceased.

But I still had his portrait, and I put it in *Andersonville* as a bookmark.

The novel, a typical sprawling Civil War epic, exuded my kind of heroics, but while some characters were authentic, most were Southern stereotypes. I'd become really well read on the Civil War by then, and when I got to Johnny Ransom, a character keeping a diary in Andersonville prison, I recognized right away that MacKinlay Kantor had lifted passages from Johnny Ransom's actual Civil War journal, which I'd read in Rice's rare books room. Since to me the cardinal sin in writing was using someone else's words without acknowledgment, I sat a long time with the book in my hands, completely unnerved.

Although I did manage to finish the book, as I put Tim's photograph inside the back cover, I couldn't help wondering what other characters, scenes, and descriptions his father might have pilfered.

I finished my M.A., Jack and I married, and I put a
writing life in New York on hold while he worked on his
Ph.D. I'd planned to teach in college, but I hated to waste
the Texas teaching certificate I'd earned along the way, so
I accepted a job in a Houston junior high on Alvera Street.
During the orientation, when the principal cautioned,
"Remember, teachers, don't turn your back on the students,"
I should have fled at once.

I didn't.

And a hellish year for all of us followed.

I'd been raised around poverty, but I didn't know this
kind of poverty in a run-down urban area with waterlogged
sofas and stained mattresses littering the vacant lots. I didn't
know the kind of chronic anger that left children frustrated
and bewildered from the time they could walk. I also didn't
know anything about junior high school students in general
since I'd been an overachiever, I'd just taught a freshman
class of Rice overachievers, and Honey, ten years my junior,
entering puberty and also destined for Rice, manfully read
every book on the reading lists I made out for her.

My students and I never came close to a truce, and
although the teachers at the school never mentioned the
word *gang*, pitched battles—both in the halls and on the
playground—occurred daily. All of the boys carried switch-
blades, and if they weren't carving their initials on desktops,
they were threatening each other, and the one time the
class stayed silent for the entire hour was the afternoon a
student, stabbed in the groin, staggered into the room, collapsed against the blackboard, and bled copiously onto the
floor until the police and the ambulance arrived.

When that school year ended, I drove across MacGregor Park to Texas Southern University, Houston's "separate but equal" black college.

In 1956 Texas, black students still couldn't enroll in white colleges. Black students could never have had the advantage of my Rice education, so it seemed logical—even moral—to take mine to them. And I'd be teaching adults, not seventh graders.

I don't know if the chairman of the English Department did more than glance at my transcript, but at the opening faculty meeting when I was introduced, I stood up and realized that despite my new surname of Esslinger, everyone in the room accepted my olive skin, dark hair, and dark eyes as a racial variation, and that they thought I, too, was black.

I'd been pinning my hair into a faux chignon and spraying it glass hard so that it did resemble a press job, I got an extremely hearty tan every summer, and since I came from Wyoming, the fact that I lacked a black accent surprised no one. So even though I never lied, I let everyone keep assuming I was black.

It was near the end of my second year before my office mate Mabel said she'd graduated from U. of Iowa and asked point-blank where I'd gone to college. I had to say, "Rice."

She told me she went home and said to her husband, Romy, "Pat went to Rice, and she— She went to Rice! She's white!"

Romy, whom I'd met many times, said, "She's still Pat, isn't she?"

When she came in the next morning, she said at once, "You're white!"

I had to nod.

"But how could you possibly pass for black? You don't even have any lips."

"I think there must be a tribe in Africa somewhere that looks like me."

I usually said it flippantly, and I never added that people generally see what they expect to see. And what would anyone at Texas Southern in segregated Houston assume I'd be but black since only African Americans taught at the all-black university?

By the time I went to Texas Southern I'd lost any preconceived notions I might have had about black students, and since they sat quietly, trying their best to make their subjects match their verbs, and since I'd realized the first day that I *could* tell them apart as easily as I'd distinguished one Rice student from another, I had no conflict with being at an all-black school. Even my mother, who of course would never tell her bridge club, accepted the fact that I taught at a black university.

I, however, had a conflict with my own guilt.

If I went alone—or with Jack, whose blond hair and light brown eyes were unmistakably Anglo—to any restaurant on Fannin, I could sit down and order. No matter how deep my tan was, if I were alone, I could try on evening gowns in Foley's.

Of course in my departmental office, I mentioned eating only at the black café on Downing Street, and I brought up in class only films showing at the black theater. But most of the city was denied to my colleagues, and that fact hung on me like a fifty-pound flak jacket. I'd let them assume something untrue, and my allowing—continuing—the mistake constituted a betrayal.

Four of us shared an office, and one of them was another new professor named Toni Wofford, who became Toni Morrison before publication of her first book.

I thought when she walked into the office that she was the most beautiful woman I'd ever encountered. She also knew so much about New York's literary scene that I had to start subscribing to the *Saturday Review* just to trail behind her.

Toni came from Cincinnati, with a degree from Howard, so she wasn't used to Texas segregation, and one day she came in the office to inform us that Grace Kelly's new film, *High Society*, was at Loews. "I want to see it, so you know what I'm going to do? I'm going to buy a maid's uniform, rent a little blond kid, and say at the ticket booth that Miss Sally asked me to take little Amanda to the movies during her bridge club."

Everyone in the office laughed.

But of course she didn't do it.

And when she suggested we check out Orson Welles's *Othello* at a tiny art theater to see if our students might enjoy it and said, "Why don't you call for tickets?" I assumed that she, like the rest of the school, accepted me as a Wyoming black with no accent.

The theater manager, thrilled that we might bring whole classes to his run-down theater, told us we'd be his guests for the screening, but when two black women showed up, he rushed us inside in pale-faced panic. We sat in the rickety seats—where four other patrons slept—and both of us started to laugh. We laughed so hard the row rocked.

Toni leaned over and whispered through her laugh, "I don't think our students would like this production after all, do you?"

In 1957, Little Rock's Central High incident shook the rest of the nation, but no one at Texas Southern discussed it, so I didn't either. I merely listened to what seemed more fascinating than the Arkansas event to both the faculty and student body—the fact that over the summer, three students had gotten pregnant by the same shiftless boy.

Two of the girls had signed up for my English class, and they sat together in the last row, stared with rapt attention when I explained a poem or a story, and giggled together while they walked into the September sunshine to cross the street to the next red brick building.

I never knew if the rumor about the same boy fathering all three babies was true, but everyone knew the girls' only options were to give birth or to get a back-room abortion. And since we also knew that their mothers, all domestic workers, would have scrimped for years—would have hoarded every dime and quarter—to send their daughters to college, it seemed only logical that the girls decided to risk the abortion.

None of us ever learned how they came by the bottle of mercuric acid they elected to use, but all three of them douched with it, and then two of them also drank it in case that was the way one aborted an embryo from one's stomach.

I knew from my biologist husband that mercuric acid was strong enough to eat through iron pipe, and when I heard about the girls' deaths, I tried not to imagine what that particular acid would do to soft tissue.

And on the rare occasions when some student asks me, "Doc, are you pro-choice or pro-life?" I always answer, "Yes."

One morning I was sitting in the office when Toni came in with a pastel drawing tacked to a board. "A wife of a professor at Houston University does portraits, and I had this done last week," she said. "I picked it up this morning on my way to school."

She happily propped the pastel against the wall and moved back so those of us in the office could view and appreciate it.

It was a full-face drawing of a pinkly sweet young woman with rosy skin and dark curly hair. The eyes were dark, but I couldn't see any expression in them. The portrait, whose features wore the nondescript blankness of middle-class whiteness, could have represented any number of my brunette Rice classmates, any number of brunette Houstonians.

Toni was beautiful because her skin shone the color of melting Hershey bars and her dark eyes—enhanced by curling lashes that nearly touched her upper lids when she blinked—held depths of understanding. She was beautiful when her nose flared slightly broader in disdain for Texans who didn't know that our students might lack backgrounds but stood as bright and graceful as students anywhere. And I was appalled that the wife of that University of Houston professor had rendered her in pale chalks as if the box lacked every variant of brown, as if the sketch were of a bland white colleague. I wished I could have done Toni in the dark browns and vermilion lip shades she deserved.

She stood approving the portrait. "I think it's just great. What do you think?"

The others in the office agreed that it was lovely, so I naturally kept quiet.

The second year I was at Texas Southern, I drove with Mabel to the Southwest Modern Language Association meeting at Baylor University in Waco.

When she and Romy picked me up in their car, she asked how she looked in her sand-colored hat and suit.

"They're a really classy shade."

She grinned. "I know that, but I asked how *I* looked in them."

She was the only person I ever met who realized I sidestepped if I didn't want to hurt someone's feelings. But since she'd asked this question directly, I had to say I'd seen her wear more becoming colors.

When we got to Baylor, Romy let us off, and we went to the auditorium. Three black faculty members from some other black college stood among the four hundred or five hundred white MLA attendees, and Mabel and I gravitated toward them at once. We five black professors didn't have to search for an afternoon acquaintanceship by running through the conversational gambits of our specialty fields, discussing which sessions we'd attend, or which table we'd selected for the luncheon that was included in the membership dues. We were black, and we intended to stick together.

Especially since not one white faculty member spoke to us the entire day.

One of those white professors, from the University of Houston, a man I'd talked to at numerous social functions when I'd been a Rice teaching assistant, stood beside a column outside the auditorium before a session, and I said hello to him.

He looked at me, then at my companions, and walked away without a word.

I'd thought Jack's master's work on establishing the life cycle of the hominivorax was wonderfully original, possibly brilliant, but when he merely elaborated on the same idea for his Ph.D. dissertation, I was a little disappointed. I'd assumed dissertations demanded a higher standard than that. And when he took a third year to finish, I began to wonder if the Biology Department might be merely ushering him out rather than demanding more of him because they couldn't deal with his drinking.

For, by the second year of our marriage, I'd realized that he, like my father, drank too much.

I'd usually joined him when he drank something with flavor, like a gimlet, or if he had a carafe of wine, but that year he developed a taste for dry martinis without ice or olives—which meant, of course, that no Vermouth, olive, or ice tainted the straight gin in his cocktail glass. If we went to a BYOL graduate student gathering, he always took a fifth of cheap vodka and always finished the bottle before we left the party. Naturally, he also always staggered and had to be helped to the car.

If we gave a student party in our little three-room garage apartment near the Rice campus, he drank his supply and then dipped into the liquors the others had brought. He usually collapsed on the bed in the tiny bedroom before everyone had gone.

I'd excused my father because I'd understood his feelings of being an extreme outsider, and now I made the same excuses for Jack. I'd noticed that his fellow students dutifully invited him to parties, but that he didn't have any real friends, and of course since he was a doctoral candidate, he was probably highly stressed.

Despite his accelerated drinking, in 1958 Jack graduated from Rice with a Ph.D. in parasitology, and it was time
for me to decide on a new career.

Since the late '50s wasn't a time for new brides to leave
husbands and go write it a garret, I hadn't applied for a New
York job. And since I hadn't yet decided how to launch
into the novel I planned to write, I bowed to convention—
which, of course, my mother smugly seconded—and agreed
to go wherever Jack decided to go.

He did have great credentials (As one friend put it
later, "He had all the tickets."), and he got offers from both
Harvard and Tulane. I hoped he'd take the job at Harvard
so I'd at least be near New York, but he said Tulane Medical
School was better for what he wanted to do.

He didn't articulate what he wanted to do, but I followed him to New Orleans, where we rented an apartment
in the Garden District with white columns and twelve-foot
ceilings that had been converted from the front parlor of a
mansion on Coliseum Street.

I'd never been in New Orleans before, and the languid,
Mississippi River–humid air was harder to breathe than the
dry heat rising from Houston's concrete freeways. New
Orleans had expensive shops and restaurants similar to
Houston's, but the sidewalks in front of New Orleans' plate-
glass windows were littered with cigarette butts and spittle,
the grocery stores were cramped into tiny spaces where
shotgun houses had once stood, and omnipresent mildew
seeped through every wall in the city.

It didn't take long for me as a history buff, however, to
fall in love with the root-splayed sidewalks and the rattling
streetcars.

Tradition draped the mansions in Uptown New
Orleans the way Spanish moss bearded the cypress trees
and dewy webs festooned the wrought-iron balconies in
the French Quarter. Amid the antebellum townhouses, the
pigeon-splattered statues of Lee and Jackson, and Lafitte's
Blacksmith Shop on Bourbon Street that served cocktails
by candlelight even in midmorning, the nineteenth century
remained the present.

I learned to appreciate the odors of ancient wood and
café au lait, the sour-mash exhale from the Mississippi, and
the not-unpleasant combination of boiling shrimp and cay-
enne. Jack was merely an instructor, so money was scarce,
but on Sundays I persuaded him to ride the St. Charles
trolley with me to Canal and stroll past the iron fences of
Jackson Square where mediocre artists hung barely recognizable sketches of Cajun swamps and garish watercolors of
Mardi Gras floats.

New Orleans sprawled from Lake Pontchartrain to the
river, an isolated and exotic oasis from the rest of America,
and much later, when my friend Kenneth started conducting literary tours of the Quarter and asked me to join him,
I was happy to convey my affection for the city. I liked telling its stories while I herded groups of Midwesterners down
Bourbon and Royal and pointed out the third-floor window
on Pirates Alley from which Faulkner shot dried peas at
mules and nuns, the Hotel de Ville where Degas learned he
couldn't paint in the lush New Orleans light, the site of the
slave auctions that so appalled Whitman, and the DESIRE
streetcar that enthralled Tennessee Williams.

Jack had always given me time and space to write, but I could compose short stories about the South for only five or six hours a day, and since I wasn't teaching, I decided that while I waited for New York and/or the hazy themes of my novel to jell, I might as well take graduate classes, which were free to faculty wives.

All grad schools at the time required the Graduate Record Exam, so I signed up for it. I had an exemplary literary background from Rice—in literature before 1900, of course, but nonetheless exemplary—and I'd taught for two years, so when I got to the exam room, I opened the timed test booklet with confidence.

Ever since that spring of the battery of high school tests, I'd distrusted multiple choice, and now as I read the four possibilities to each GRE question, I realized I'd been right. The answers were not only predictable but simplistic. The testing center had agreed on which novels were great, which characters were significant, which plot lines merited unraveling. There was no room for deviation, no room for creative thinking. I knew that academics—with no quibbling—deemed Southey inferior to Byron, considered Joyce better than Stephens or O'Faolain, valued Sterne over Trollope, so I could choose the right As, the proper Bs or Cs without hesitation.

I finished the test early.

And even though I had less faith than ever in multiple-choice exams, I ended up with a score high enough for any university in the country.

I'd still rather have gone to Harvard, but since I was in New Orleans, I decided Tulane would do.

I had no intention of going for a doctorate, and I went on campus only to take leisurely classes, listen to leisurely lectures, and get in the mood to write my novel.

But I'd learned the academic game too well, and by spring, I'd taken all the courses I needed. I found myself almost automatically reading for the Ph.D. comprehensive exams.

The other seven graduate students taking the exams had been at Tulane for years, and when my friend Jim Young, the one who'd given me the spelling test and who now had a Rice Ph.D., joined the Tulane English Department that same year, one of the other professors murmured, "If anyone fails the comprehensives, it'll be Pat Esslinger. No one knows who she is."

Jim looked at him. "That's right. You don't know her. She won't fail."

I didn't. And by the end of the year, I was writing a dissertation on Sean O'Casey, who reminded me of my stubbornly just and pug-nosed Irish father. I'd been drawn to O'Casey since I'd read his early Abbey plays and his memoir, *I Knock at the Door*, and I knew exactly what I wanted to say about his work.

I wrote to him in Devon and received a letter back immediately in which he either gave thoughtful answers to my questions or a thoughtful, "Not as I knows on."

The dissertation flowed to quick completion, my defense lasted forty-six minutes, and in the steaming August heat of 1960 I received a Ph.D. from Tulane.

The other grad students nicknamed me "The Mythical Beast."

My mother had never really warmed up to Jack,
but she did like to visit New Orleans. She liked the lavish
antique emporia on Royal ("We're just looking, thank you.")
and the cheap, secondhand stores on Magazine down by
the river, where shoppers had to be more creative ("Don't
you think I can cover that Victorian chair with brocade
to match the Queen Anne sofa?"). I took her for gumbo
on Esplanade and to Fitzgerald's, overlooking the lake, for
seasonal fried soft-shelled crabs. She also liked elegant tea
rooms—I was sure she wanted to be mistaken for visiting
Irish or British royalty—so I usually hunted up one of those
before she flew over from Houston.

We went to movies, and I took her shopping at department stores on Canal. I remember vividly the time in
Maison Blanche when she insisted I buy a scarlet teddy
nightgown. "You look good in red and you have nice legs.
You know Jack will like it."

That afternoon, however, when Jack came in from the
medical school, she quickly changed into the little red
nightgown and fluttered to the living room to show him,
the store tags still flickering from the sleeves. I heard her
murmur from the next room, "Isn't this sexy? Now don't
look at the price, just appreciate the color."

When she scurried back to the bedroom to shed the
little gown, she whispered, "I hope I didn't spoil it for you. I
wouldn't want Jack to see *me* in it every time you wear it."

I realized that while she knew she was beautiful and
knew I wasn't, she nonetheless couldn't resist competing
with me. So of course I would never have mentioned her
clotted thighs, her blue-veined calves, or her neck that had
the beginnings of a turkey wattle.

Honey liked to come to New Orleans, too, I think mostly because it had such a reputation for voodoo and witchcraft. When she came, we toured the cemeteries scattered around the French Quarter and Garden District and studied the upright crypts that oozed green slime no matter what the season. We stopped by the house at 1140 Royal, whose 1830s mistress had kept an attic full of slaves whom she tortured to death while grand dinner parties were in progress downstairs. Since so many slaves died on the top floor and an occasional slave fell from the roof in an escape attempt, that house alone created a whole host of wraiths.

New Orleans, of course, abounded with the preternatural anyway, and when I first got my Ph.D. and started teaching "The Wasteland" at Dillard University, I'd seen a deck of Tarot cards in a shop window. I'd gone in to get them to help the students visualize Eliot's images in the Tarot passages.

The shop owner, gazing at me from water-colored eyes, sat behind the counter with a Siamese cat perched on his shoulder. The cat had pale irises of nearly the same colorless hue, and he watched with his owner as I crossed the room.

"I'd like to buy those Tarot cards in the window. How much are they?"

The pair looked at me a long moment before the man, and perhaps the cat, shook his head. "I won't sell them to you. You should never touch Tarot cards."

I accepted his pronouncement the way I'd accepted the billboard.

But when I took Honey into his shop, the pale-eyed owner didn't hesitate. He nodded, took her fifteen dollars, and handed over the pack of cards.

I'd waived the heroic factor because Jack had been bright, funny—and handsome.

Very soon, however, I'd realized that despite his appreciation of my writing ("This story breaks me up.") and his blond good looks, he resorted to jokes to avoid having to deal with intimacy. After a couple of martinis, he repeated elaborate stories that ended in puns ("Never stow thrones in grass houses.") and prevented listeners from interjecting anything personal, anything that might approach real emotion.

By then I knew about his unhappy childhood—how his father had insisted he go out for sports ("I didn't want to play ball. All I wanted to do was look at microbes in a bottle of water."), and how his mother had used him as a surrogate husband ("She thought only of herself, and when I was home she insisted she was ill, that I pay attention just to her."). I sympathized when his college roommate told me that any time Jack's parents came for visits, Jack would hide in the closet until they left the campus. But it also dawned on me that he was much like his mother, so preoccupied with his own injuries that he rarely noticed anyone else's, and I saw drinking as his attempt to dull the pain.

I established a crammed schedule of preparing for and teaching three classes, writing fiction and scholarly articles, occasionally painting, caring for my two little girls—born in 1959 and 1961—and creating gourmet dinners, which I often served to ten or twenty guests, but no amount of compartmentalizing on my part quite disguised Jack's increasing fondness for dry martinis.

Finally, the medical school noticed the anesthetizing martinis, and in an attempt to wean Jack from nightly stops at Lafitte's, the faculty arranged for him to go to a newly opened branch facility in Cali, Colombia, to study jungle parasites and to teach Colombian doctors about parasitical infections. I took my two little girls and went along.

Cali contained great wealth and greater poverty, and with the dawning of the Peace Corps, the city teemed with college kids who came with idealistic projects for building bridges between Red and Blue villages or for teaching mothers to diaper their babies. Their projects were mostly doomed from the start because the Colombian poor lacked both cloth for diapers and potable water, and Red and Blue villages were hacking each other to pieces with machetes. And while we waited in a pension for a house to come vacant, I listened to the enthusiasm and wondered if all Peace Corps volunteers were equally naïve.

Cali was perfect for me, however, and allowed me to churn out manuscript after manuscript.

I was invited to every party given by the English-speaking colony, the British wives welcomed me to their Thursday English teas, and I also gave birth to a son at the Valle del Cauca Hospital—whom I named after Sean O'Casey. But because all foreigners hired maids to walk children and guard the three-story houses from thieves, I had more time than ever to write.

While in Cali, I did finish dozens of short stories and at last my first full-length manuscript, a historical novel set in 1815 Cartagena.

I'd gone to Colombia knowing little South American history, but all of us from *los Estados Unidos* found ourselves in a crash course on the *violencia*—that bewildering civil war that by 1960 had killed 350,000 Colombians—and as I read about the current violence, I went through volumes of Colombian history and became intrigued by the nineteenth-century Spanish war that had also decimated the country.

Bolívar had led Latin America's rebellion against Spanish rule, but by 1815, Spain was determined to retake her straying South American colonies. The opening salvo was the order for Spanish ships to blockade—and starve into submission—the walled city of Cartagena, which Spain had spent millions in gold and two centuries fortifying.

The siege would be the background of my novel.

Unfortunately, I prided myself on being able to write any incident—as George Williams in my single creative writing course had taught—whether or not I'd experienced it. And I accepted the creative writing truism that a talented storyteller could effectively use any point of view, including that of the heroic revolutionary Santiago Stuart or the Cartagena wife with whom he had an affair.

I believed as well that a "real" writer could render any setting—whether or not she or he had ever seen the place. So writing with a pen on a yellow pad in the study of my three-story house in Cali, I created 1815 Cartagena without having been in that particular port city.

Colombia in the 1960s was a strange place for foreigners, and in Cali, we found ourselves in a tropical valley surrounded by death.

The hills beyond the city rose arid and stark, but in residential areas no tree or bank of trumpet flowers seemed to wilt. Shrubs could have been fashioned of chartreuse plastic, palms seemed to produce fronds, blossoms, and yellow-green bananas all at the same time, and in upper-class Colombian homes we could walk from the master bath onto a lush green lawn (protected by twelve-foot walls embedded with glass to keep beggars out). The valley contained no dangerous insects, and every lavish mansion had open squares on each floor to let daily rains fall straight through the roof and down three floors to the basement drain.

But at least a dozen beggars died every night in the slum of Ciloé, and the *violencia* essentially jailed us below a hill of three not-quite-straight crosses. Although no foreigner had yet been killed, *El Tiempo* contained daily photos of massacres, and any American or Briton driving the dry roads had to use the kind of transportation Tulane supplied Jack: a white Jeep with—somehow ominous—red crosses on the doors and roof.

The eternal spring and the hovering mortality intertwined to infect the entire foreign population with palpable sexual tension, and the real possibility of extramarital affairs—those "Colombian adventures" newcomers somehow anticipated as soon as they arrived on Avianca—loomed omnipresent in the American and British colonies.

8 & 7

Foreign husbands—usually salesmen or engineers—often camped at the Calima dam site or stayed in hotels in Bogotá for days at a time, so despite the country club dances that occurred weekly, and the vodka that could be added to *jugo de naranja* at ten in the morning, daylight hours still dragged for foreign wives with too many maids, cooks, gardeners, and seamstresses. In the general ennui, no one seemed exempt from the lure of adultery, and one afternoon, Amy, a close American friend, asked if I liked her husband well enough to take him as a lover.

"What?"

"When you and he drove out to Buga that time to hunt for artifacts, I thought maybe you were having an affair."

I didn't want to disparage her husband by saying he wasn't my type, and I said, "We both like ancient pottery, but come on, Amy, you have to know we're just friends."

"Actually he's a real romantic, and I thought as long as we were down here in a foreign country, away from home and all, and there's so much drinking and sex around, he could get an affair out of his system. He's never had one, you know."

Nor did I want to shred her belief in my sophistication by confessing that I'd never had an affair either, so I murmured, "I've just never thought of Tom as a lover."

"That's too bad actually. He idealizes women, and I thought if he realized that brilliant, heroine types like you perspired and had to brush their teeth, he might give up that sort of nonsense and settle for me."

As a romantic myself, I did consider an affair.

But I'd grown up on Jane Austen and movies that insisted love and living happily ever after were the norm. And although this was the '60s, it wasn't yet the pot-smoking-free-love-open-marriage '60s, and the weight of literature—with dire warnings from Tolstoy and Flaubert—still considered adultery a refuge of the miserable.

All the great books also agreed that people could change. And while I didn't articulate it in bald terms, I somehow tacitly decided that I had to give Jack a chance.

When I'd first met him, he'd waxed lyrical about parasitology, the biological science that threaded the others together—vertebrates hosting invertebrates which in turn harbored viruses and bacteria—but by the time he'd gotten his Ph.D., I'd realized he couldn't synthesize. He'd become a taxonomist who took scrupulous notes on unknown species but who then merely catalogued his findings. I hadn't insisted on an authentic "hero" who observes and is kind, but I had thought I'd married someone creative.

But what kind of woman could justify swapping men just because the one she married fell short of being creative?

Still, the image of an affair lingered. And I might have sifted through the men amenable to becoming my lover, might even have chosen one if he'd displayed unusual heroism. But heroics seemed in short supply in the early 1960s, and I again crowded my days with writing, researching, directing maids and children, and attending parties.

All of which resounded with a terrible sameness.

As a child tramping the Wyoming hills, I'd valued
flint slices worked by ancient Native Americans into bird
points, and pebbles hand-drilled and polished to bead a
necklace. So as soon as I arrived in the arid Colombian
landscape chock-full of pre-Columbian artifacts, I began studying ancient pottery while I wrote and attended
American parties and English teas. And after a while I could
identify authentic bowls and authentic clay *caciques* sporting
gold nose rings in their clay nostrils.

I discovered which Cali shopkeepers were fences for
grave robbers, which shops paid poverty-stricken *campesinos*
a few centavos for jade carved into an owl or dog amulet,
and whenever I could, I took the artifacts home. I'd naturally heard the archaeological arguments that collectors
expand the market for looted grave goods, but at the same
time, I knew *huaqueros* often dug up burials and smashed clay
masks for the turquoise inlays, that tourists took ancient
pottery home as junk, and if I saw in a dusty shop a tiny
pre-Columbian monkey with folded paws and a tail curved
over one shoulder, I couldn't risk its destruction or its con-
signment to a toy box, so I bought it.

Jack developed an interest in artifacts as well, and after
a few months, we could both distinguish genuine funereal
vases from modern fakes. Our Cali acquaintances beamed
at us, the happy American couple with such an entwined
consuming interest.

But alcohol was even more plentiful in Cali than ancient
art. Smugglers brought in monthly shipments of contraband
Beefeaters, Cutty Sark, and Benedictine, while Colombians
themselves bottled cheap, licorice-flavored "water with
teeth," *aguardiente.*

And Jack's drinking got worse.

It was once a rather macabre party game—and later a prompt for creative writing workshops—to ask, "Do you remember where you were on November 22, 1963?"

I was walking on a street just off the Plaza Caycedo.

It was a typical sunny day, and beggars wearily meandered the sidewalks the way the contaminated water in the Rio Cali flowed sluggishly through the city. Americans had been cautioned not to give even one centavo to a beggar. ("You'll be marked. They'll swarm around you ten deep every time you leave the house. Remember, you can't make a dent in the poverty of the 130,000 poor living in Ciloé.")

I stepped over the extended legs of a beggar with elephantiasis *("Perdón, señor.")* while I noticed he'd painted the sore on his gigantically swollen calf with some bright gentian violet antiseptic.

I'd spent the day in the library and had missed the shortwave news I usually heard while I sipped a Bristol Cream with the Canadian wife next door, so I was dumbfounded when Caleño businessmen and maids, carrying briefcases or market baskets on their way from the *mercado*, came up and grabbed my hands. I suppose Colombians could always spot an American, and after they explained the Dallas tragedy in English or Spanish, they asked uneasily if *norteamericanos* would now revolt the way Colombians always revolted after a *presidente* had been assassinated.

My Spanish was inadequate to explain the constitution of *los Estados Unidos* that provided for such contingencies as assassinations, and I could only shake my head as I accepted their condolences, pressed their hands, and murmured, *"Gracias."*

My daughters, Stephanie and Shelley, had been born
in a New Orleans hospital with all the required anesthe-
siologists, obstetricians, attending nurses, and antiseptic
precautions. Sean was born in a Cali hospital, delivered by
a Colombian doctor, fresh from the country club course
and wearing a butter-yellow golf shirt with gray Italian
silk slacks and cleated, tasseled shoes. The single nurse in
attendance hadn't donned scrubs, and as she wheeled me
into the delivery room, I could only hope she'd washed her
hands.

The doctor, whom I'd met at many elaborate parties
given by the Colombian canning company Fruco, didn't
offer an anesthetic as he chatted about the upcoming bullfights. "Every year they bring the best toreros from Spain,
and this *feria* season, Paco Camino is coming. Are you fond
of the *corridas?*"

I hated to appear impolite, hated to interrupt or ask for
an anesthetic, which the hospital might not have, so I nodded. And had the baby while completely, fully awake.

But that did give me a writer's opportunity to observe
the whole process, from the being-cut-in-half labor pains to
the emerging baby flecked with blood. I was unpleasantly
surprised—stunned actually—to learn that labor continues
until the uterus expels the placenta. I'd never read in any
book or seen on the screen in any romantic comedy the
slightest hint that birth wasn't finished as soon as the baby
arrived.

I could also document that a newborn remains the pale
waxy color of a cheap candle until it takes a breath. I saw
that only as oxygen rushed through the inflated lungs and
coursed through the veins and arteries did the little body
wash pink.

I hadn't known that oxygen alone made all the difference.

The obstetrician who delivered Sean had been trained in U.S. hospitals, and when I went back for my postbirth six-week checkup, he insisted on doing what other American doctors often did. "I'll just cauterize to clean everything up."

In the process, he unfortunately burned through a vein. And I began to bleed.

Copiously.

After a couple of weeks, I called to say that I was still bleeding, but he said just to stay in bed and everything would be fine in a few days.

Friends took the children to the country club—which I could never bring myself to join—the maid, Herlinda, joyfully accepted care of the new baby, *un varón*, and other friends came over to teach me how to play chess and bridge while lying prone.

I kept bleeding.

My complexion turned gray, and the Canadian wife next door said later that she'd been certain I'd be dead in another two weeks.

At last Jack noticed and took me back to the hospital in the white Jeep.

Perhaps because Jack was on the hospital staff, or perhaps just because he was a male, the doctor listened and then said casually, "I didn't know it was this bad."

Finally he repeated the cauterization and created enough scar tissue to stopper the vein, but the experience didn't endear the Valle del Cauca Hospital to me.

In Colombia, I decided once again not to meet an author, the Nadaist, Gonzalo Arango.

An Argentinean directed the Valle del Cauca Hospital, and his wife, who knew Arango, asked if I wanted to fly to Bogotá to meet him. I had to say, *"Gracias, pero no."*

This time I *did* like his work and I'd penned translations of a number of his stories. I was also well read on the Nadaistas, a group of young male, very macho, and very vocal writers who saw the nothingness in Colombian life and the madness in the *violencia*. So this time my refusal to meet a famous author came from another cause.

While I could translate Spanish on paper and make a story readable in English, I was a disaster at speaking the language. I'd spent my entire first year in Colombia studying Spanish, but my accent was hopelessly American, my syntax was impaired, and I still couldn't carry on a decent conversation. A friend once asked, "How can you know so much Spanish and speak it so badly?" And I knew that if I met Arango, I'd come off as a simpleton. Since I was also a mother of three (I'd observed that motherhood was a role scorned in macho Colombia for any woman but the Virgin Mary.), I wouldn't be able to hold my own with a fierce young contemporary, angry and nihilistic, writer.

So I decided to protect my own ego.

Even though *The Paris Review* said they'd publish my translated story if I got permission from the author, I didn't go to Bogotá to meet Gonzalo Arango.

And of course, I also passed up my chance to be published in *The Paris Review*.

For three years, one of my favorite shops in Cali was Schmidt's Jewelry.

My father, with his background—whatever it actually was—didn't trust his own taste, so during my childhood, I had scouted jewelry stores for him. He'd turned down emeralds as too breakable and gold as too malleable, but now in Colombia, with the dollar at ten pesos, I decided to buy some soft gold as well as some friable Muso emeralds, and I went to Schmidt's. His shop fronted the Plaza Caycedo, near the squat, yellow church from which the priests had stripped the gold leaf to feed the poor of Ciloé. The priests had replaced the once-gold haloes with blue neon, so few Caleños—and no tourists—ever went inside. When they passed up the church, they invariably stopped at Schmidt's.

Herr Schmidt spoke English with an emphatic Belgian accent, *not* German ("I come from Antwerp, *mi señora*."), and when I admired a gold scorpion pin in his case, he said fiercely, "Ex-Nazis buy that. *Por favor*, I beg you not to touch it."

I kept going back to see the eighteen-karat scorpion, made by the lost-wax process of pouring molten gold into the mold of an actual scorpion, but he refused to sell it to me. "You must not have it, my lovely Señora. You should avoid all connection to Nazis."

"It's such a beautiful piece."

"At least wait until the Nazis leave in 1965. Nineteen sixty-five makes the twenty-year amnesty for minor war crimes, and the criminals will go. After that you can consider buying it."

I did wait, and in January 1965 I stopped by the shop to get the pin.

His assistant shook his head. "I am sorry, Señora. Herr Schmidt has left for Germany. He said that twenty years of exile in this wretched country was enough."

Jack played jazz clarinet with piercing intensity, and while I tried to convince myself that the clarinet was his way of being creative, he had to be staggering drunk before he could pick it up. When he did play at Cali festivals, however, his gold hair and long-lashed brown eyes made him seem very young, and despite his reeling, every visiting American who heard his clarinet invariably asked why Cali's American high school didn't form an orchestra around such a talented student.

He wore black berets for stage appearances, and since he also liked to tango in tight black pants, we never missed a costume ball in either the American or the British colony. I'd been wearing costumes all my life, so I usually just put a shell comb in my hair and draped it with a mantilla, but he researched—in the minimal library and meager bookstore—what Lafayette wore and how Gandhi tucked his robes. Caleño seamstresses were willing to try anything— even three-cornered hats—and Jack needed only boots for the former or a white sheet, wire glasses, and grease to slick his hair flat for the latter to look authentic.

I realized, of course, that the improvised music and improvised clothes let him dissemble—the way he hid behind the interminable puns and the martinis—and become a person he could stand, a person other people might be able to stand.

The medical school—and I in particular—had hoped that Cali would affect some miracle cure, but that hadn't happened.

And Jack retreated deeper into alcohol.

My nod to the obstetrician as he discussed the *corridas* had been a nod of politeness, but it was also more than that. I *did* like bullfights.

I never felt really at home in Cali; I could never come to terms with the inherent machismo of the culture, and the language with its shrugging acceptance, *se cayó* ("it just fell"), lacked too much cause-and-effect for my American realism. But when it came to the heroics of the bullring, the Spanish audience, Hemingway, and I meshed.

At my first afternoon of the six-day *corridas*, I fell under the spell of the ritual. I loved the pageantry, the *pasadobles*, the skill of the toreros who controlled a ferocious animal with a swirling pink and gold *capote* or a small crimson *muleta*. I embraced the allegory and accepted that the gleaming sable bulls represented compelling dark forces, that stunning young men, glittering in rhinestone-encrusted Suits of Light, could symbolize all that was brave. The bullfight was the one occasion in Colombia I felt comfortable enough to shout "Bravo!" and join the crowds as they surged to their feet and waved white kerchiefs for a brilliant *muleta* pass or howled down a sloppy kill that required a dozen stabs to finish the bull.

And although I never said it to one of the stolid Americans eating prawns from silver trays or catching champagne from the sparkling fountain at a Fruco party, I never forgave them for calling the *corrida* a "sport" and rooting for the bull. I never forgave them for not making a distinction between a beautiful, slender young man and a male bovine, for not realizing the latter could win only if the former died.

After three years in Cali, we returned to New Orleans, and I began sending out my Colombian stories.

The first I had accepted, "Candelaria Project—Progress Report," was taken by *The Southern Review*, and its acceptance came about—as Jim Dickey foresaw—because I'd become acquainted with one of the editors.

It was a story based on an incident I'd heard from a female physician, but when I wrote it, I'd changed the protagonist to a male—as I was in the habit of doing no matter what the subject. That same month I submitted another story, a Wyoming one entitled "The Life and Death of a Roustabout," which also had a male protagonist. *The Kansas Quarterly* editor wrote back to say he was hesitating over it. He asked if I'd been published in any other literary magazines, and when I said *The Southern Review* had just taken a story, he immediately accepted the new one.

It was obviously a combination of "who you know" and "who publishes you."

When "Candelaria Project" came out, I had the shock of getting a letter from the McIntosh & Otis Literary Agency asking if I'd let them represent me. I hadn't thought about a literary agent, and I didn't know that the agency asking for me had also represented Steinbeck. But I agreed to give them a try, and I sent a story.

They didn't have immediate luck placing it, and all my colleagues and Jack badgered me until I wrote that I wanted to try another agent who was a better salesman.

I had no idea how hard it might be to get another agent or how impossible it would be to get McIntosh & Otis back.

I sometimes thought that under the right circumstances my mother could have been Josef Mengele. I never saw her shocked, never saw her react with either rage or high glee, and her flirting always held a thread of disdain. But I'd seen her use frigid withdrawal, and I knew that deep down she had the same unnerving scientific objectivity Mengele displayed when he experimented on Jewish twins in death camp laboratories.

One afternoon I'd been in the kitchen when a glass canister of sugar cracked apart in her hands and slashed her forearm. Blood welled along the slice and fell, drilling scarlet holes in the mound of sugar on the floor, but she gazed at it as indifferently as she'd gazed on my childhood nosebleeds. After five minutes of showing no emotion except interest in the blood flow, she wrapped a tea towel over her arm and left the kitchen. When she returned, a line of Band-Aids held the crimson lips of the gash together.

She showed the same cold curiosity the time she was shopping with me and volunteered to push two-year-old Sean in a grocery cart. Sean had older sisters who interpreted his silent gestures, so he didn't talk. That afternoon in the grocery store, I went to find his favorite oatmeal, and as I came around the aisle where I'd left my mother with him, I saw her jerk the cart so he'd fall forward into the metal handle.

I knew she wasn't irritated by his silence and that she was merely conducting an experiment to see what might make him speak. Banging into the handle didn't elicit a sound, and he looked at her silently while the tears flowed and I lifted him from the cart.

In the emergency room, a resident sewed four stitches in his baby lip.

I already knew the motivation for the "accident," so I never mentioned it.

Back in New Orleans, Jack continued to drink more than ever.

We rented a little house on State Street, owned by Tulane, that was within walking distance of the kids' elementary school and two blocks from the Freret bus line, and each night when he came home from the medical school and had one cocktail, he sank immediately into drunkenness. He stared blankly at the TV screen, laughed at meaningless pauses, and rarely made it through dinner. I thought perhaps he'd become so allergic to alcohol that soon he'd have to give it up.

But then he started waking about 3:00 a.m., weaving into the den where we had a small bar equipped with liqueurs and specialty drinks for parties, and slugging down two quick shot glasses of blackberry brandy or peppermint schnapps.

On one predawn forage, apparently still inebriated from that evening's whiskey sour, he staggered and dropped face first onto the walnut bar top.

When I woke up in the morning, he still sat on the floor behind the bar, but the bleeding had stopped, and the jagged gash in his forehead had begun to dry.

I helped him wash off the blood, and when he looked in the mirror, he said, "It's too late to have it stitched up. It's scabbing over. I'll just say I ran into a door."

The deep cut marred his handsomeness, but he didn't seem to notice—or care.

He continued to get up in the middle of the night until he finished off the Benedictine and Grand Marnier. I never replenished them, but he didn't seem to notice that either and merely brought home a bottle of 100-proof alcohol from the lab.

I decided the time had come for him to change, for him to acknowledge his alcoholism, and I approached a friend in the Psychiatry Department, who gave me the name of a colleague charging only fifty dollars an hour for faculty members.

Jack went to him for a year without showing any perceptible alteration, and I finally made an appointment to check the lack of progress.

"I don't discuss patients with a spouse," the psychiatrist, a hugely obese man with small feet—and obvious addiction problems himself—said primly. He settled deep in his chair and imprinted his bulk more indelibly on the leather. "But I can say that he did have an unhappy childhood."

I almost said he could have found that out by the third session, but I didn't, and he stared at me a long moment before he cleared his throat. "But while you're here, I'd like to know if he's told you what he thinks about you at parties."

I shook my head and braced myself.

By then Jack became comatose before the end of any party, either one we'd gone to or one we'd given, and I speculated that his desperation to escape himself, his life—and me—had multiplied the need for the dry martinis.

"He says you're the most beautiful woman in the room."

Given my mother and Ellen, I was more vulnerable to that than I'd thought, and I couldn't speak for a second. But finally, I was able to ask, "What about his alcoholism?"

He stared. "Alcoholism! He doesn't drink!" And he added in his prim innocence, "In fact, he told me that no one in his family can tolerate alcohol."

By 1965 the newly opened **University of New Orleans** took black as well as white students, so I could teach there without feeling segregation's residual guilt. But since by then most of the UNO faculty had also graduated from Tulane, I could be hired only part-time. The head of the department did let me teach what I wanted, however, and I had a class of African American literature, an introduction to modern drama, and a class of creative writing.

It was in teaching the last that I finally learned how to write.

One evening, while struggling with a story—trying to conjure up my male protagonist's thoughts—I was interrupted by a student who came to the door with a late paper. "I know this was due a week ago," he said, "but I just finished it."

I sighed. "OK, go in the library, and I'll get us a couple of beers to make this as painless as possible."

When I came back with two sweating beer cans, he was sitting at my desk, typing the thoughts of the protagonist without hesitating. I stood there looking at him, and in a lightning flash of epiphany I saw that of course he knew what a male would think. He *was* a male. At the same time, no matter how talented he was, he'd never know what a woman really thought or felt.

But I could tell him with absolute certainty those thoughts and feelings.

I left the library and called a writer friend. "I have a chance to be great!"

She listened to my insight, and half an hour later she appeared with a bottle of champagne. "Hey, I know when to celebrate."

Finally, I could no longer wait for the fifty-dollar-an-hour sessions to disclose Jack's avoidance of the truth. So I told him he had to give up alcohol.

I didn't insist on AA, but I did say that if he continued to drink, I'd have to leave.

He looked at me with his liquid brown eyes. "I understand."

And for the next week, he came in from the six o'clock bus and fixed me a drink without making one for himself. "I picked up bourbon and absinthe on the way home to make you a sazerac."

He sat across from me in the den and watched me sip the smoky-topaz-colored drink. He'd even added a twist of lemon peel.

He never looked away, and my questions languished as he watched the level in the tumbler. His stare was unnerving, but I knew he was trying to do what I'd asked so I didn't suggest he go watch TV with the kids or that he take one of my archaeology books (the one thing I ever saw him read) from the shelf.

But by the fifth evening of his mixing a drink and studying me as I drank it, I realized he was, either consciously or unconsciously, making the drinks stronger and stronger, that he was, either consciously or unconsciously, edging me toward alcoholism.

And I was drinking alone.

"I've decided I'll wait for a party to have a cocktail," I said. "You don't have to fix me one. I don't think it's good for you to handle alcohol."

"I don't mind."

"I know you don't. But I've decided I'd rather wait."

The next party we attended was given by a med school couple, and while I had drinks with the rest of the guests, Jack said, "I'm on the wagon," and asked for a Coke.

"Are you sure you don't want a splash of bourbon in that Coke?"

Jack shook his head.

"Come on. One drink won't hurt you. How about a beer?"

As Jack continued to shake his head, the host continued to cajole him to accept something alcoholic.

For the first time I'd noticed how someone sober in the room can make everyone else uncomfortable, but I was proud of Jack's refusing. And I was proud of myself for insisting on the sacrifice that might even make him heroic.

After a while, the men gathered in the kitchen to discuss the repairs at Charity Hospital, and the wives—just as if it were still the '50s—talked about children, New Orleans maids, and hors d'oeuvres recipes. A couple of them, who remembered I wrote, asked what I was working on.

At eleven, I went to the kitchen to get Jack.

His eyes were bleared and his mouth was slack, and I recognized that he'd held out against a drink only until he'd leaned against the refrigerator.

I glared at the host. "We have to go now."

I took Jack's arm and led him on rubbery legs toward the door, and a friend followed us in his car so he could carry Jack into the house when we reached State Street.

Even though I still resembled my father, as I got older I realized I was looking more and more like my mother. Our hands, our "good" legs in stockings and high heels, the way we held our chins, could have been interchangeable, and a clerk once looked at us standing together, riffling through the junior dresses of a department store, and said, "I can certainly see that you're mother and daughter."

I'd tried hard not to become my mother, tried hard not to demand the center spotlight and everyone's absolute attention, tried not to hoard diamonds and compliments. But perhaps we can't outrun our genes. I could limit myself to one meal a day and maintain the weight I had in college, I could give up hard liquor and confine myself to drinking only wine—in someone else's company. But when a friend said, "I love the way you give people that 'blink, blink' innocent stare when you want them to do something for you," I realized I'd gotten that from my mother.

And I also discovered that I, too, liked to perform.

I didn't try to be the extemporaneous storyteller she was; I rehearsed my notes, my asides—and my jokes—for every class, even the freshman comp classes I'd taught dozens of times. But when I'd prepared for a class, and it came off the way I planned, with class participation and all eyes on me, I found the waves of deference intoxicating, irresistible.

And because I probably needed the added bonus, I let myself believe that affection as well flowed toward me at the front of the room.

When my mother began battling cancer in Houston,
I drove over from New Orleans twice a month to listen to
her.

She told all her favorites and often repeated the story
of how she came back to Grass Creek from Denver at
eighteen just as a barnstorming flyer passed through. He
charged five dollars to take oilfield workers up for a few
minutes in his biplane, and everyone in town turned out.
My mother, who always included in the story that she was
too beautiful not to be noticed wherever she went, attracted
the handsome pilot. After the paying customers had their
turns in the air, he asked if she'd like a complimentary ride.

She naturally said yes, and as they careened through
the thin mountain air, he shouted, "Did you know it was my
plane that flew the Dempsey-Firpo fight pictures from New
York to California?"

"I'm impressed," she shouted back.

That probably did impress her since she said that particular boxing match was the most important of the decade,
but as usual, sarcasm would have dripped from her words,
and by the time they landed, the handsome aviator would
have been completely smitten.

He nonetheless flew off.

Just before she entered the hospital for the last time,
I went with her to *The Spirit of St. Louis*, and when Jimmy
Stewart, starring as Lindbergh, announced that his plane
had flown the film canister of the Dempsey-Firpo fight
across the continent, my mother cried, "Good grief!" and
turned to me in the dark theater. "I flew with Charles Lindbergh! If I'd known that's who he was, I might not have let
Anne have him."

On one of my Houston trips, my father heard that his mother had died from a heart attack. She'd been so huge at the end that she could no longer carry her bulk around with the help of a cane and had taken to a wheelchair. None of us had seen her after that 1930s summer at her house in Seattle, and as my father laid the letter on the table, he said, "I should mourn, but I can't seem to feel anything."

I was relieved he'd expressed what I was thinking, since the only emotion I felt was the uneasiness that I carried her propensity to obesity.

In the same month, my mother got a call from Ellen's fourth husband, Sherman, with the news that Ellen, too, had died.

I'd seen her around Sherm once, and she'd treated him with the same withering contempt she'd used on Ed ("Not that plate, you idiot. Get the one with the gold rim."). But my mother said he'd wept and had told her how much he'd loved Ellen.

A few months after he sent a box of Ellen's things, including her birth certificate and the purple glass Tom-and-Jerry set she'd used for Christmas eggnog, my mother called to say that a Kerrville neighbor had sent word that Sherm had also died. He'd gone every day to scrub down Ellen's headstone in the cemetery, spending all his time tending her grave, and my mother, pleased, added, "I guess he just couldn't live without her."

Both my grandmothers had been strong, both had attracted other people—especially men—and both should have been models for characters who are doers and never victims.

But I couldn't stand them, and I knew I'd never use either as a protagonist.

"Are you ever attracted to your undergraduates?"

Kenneth, the colleague with whom I conducted Quarter literary tours, Evans, and I sat in Miller Williams's motel room at the Four Cs English Conference, and since I knew Evans had addressed the question to Miller and Kenneth, I didn't say that sometimes male students could be extremely attractive. I merely silently sipped my gin and tonic.

Kenneth was gay and Miller had married a student himself, so I don't remember what either of them said, but it really didn't matter since I could tell Evans had used the question to introduce the topic of his own students, one of whom had sent him a Christmas card with a lighted candle rising from a bed of holly and red satin bows. "Do you think she had any idea how phallic a symbol a candle is?"

I hadn't met Evans before, but I'd known Miller for a couple of years as editor of *The New Orleans Review*. And as we waited for the banquet to start, and Evans and Kenneth got up to replenish our drinks, Miller murmured in a voice too low to carry across the motel room, "I don't mind refusing a story from you, Pat. You're a professional. I know you'll speak to me the next time we meet." He nodded toward Evans and lowered his voice even more. "I'm never sure about him."

I took it as a compliment, but, of course, I wished he hadn't felt obligated to send the rejection slips.

But the stories of mine he'd seen had all been written from the wrong point of view, so it was probably just as well he hadn't published any.

When my mother died after her long bout with cancer, I stood at the foot of her hospital bed.

I'd sent my father, who'd been keeping her alive by sheer force of his need to keep her alive, home to rest while I stayed with her, and she apparently seized the opportunity before he could drive back to the hospital.

Her last glance held a fiercely satisfied expression—the way people are strangely pleased to bear disaster news—and as I stood beside her, I realized how people die.

Not only do they know they're dying, but their fingers claw out to grasp one last handful of life, their faces age to those of ninety-year-olds in seconds—as if life must run its course in order for the body to die—and when the breath stops, their eyes open slightly to reveal a white porcelain rim of cornea, and the body becomes the tallow shade of a newborn.

I realized that without air, birth and death are exactly the same.

And that everyone dies alone.

I, too, would die as my mother had. Alone. And I knew at that moment that what I had with Jack wasn't enough.

In the Houston hospital room, I wasn't ready to plan the rest of my life, however, and I decided that if I could immerse myself in fiction, I wouldn't have to think about what I was going to do just yet.

So I decided to fly to Cartagena.

I'd listened to my mother's fabrications all my life, and I'd protected her feelings by not challenging anything she said. But with her death, I no longer had to hear other people's fictions. I'd been released from that protection. It was time to infuse my own stories with as much truth as I could.

I understood now that the only way to reach the truth—and be an author worth reading—was to be a writer who mined personal events, who experienced settings, and who infused a narrative with her own point of view.

So I got a plane ticket from New Orleans to Miami, then an Avianca flight to Cartagena.

Avianca flew the Miami-Cartagena run, to and from the city, only on Saturdays, which meant I'd stay a week, so I booked a room at a modest hotel inside the old town, opposite the Casa de la Inquisición, and explored the city while I rewrote the novel I'd written two years before.

But this time the characters, the births and deaths, the sky, the sand outside the walls, the rusting cannons, the stone-paved carriage streets, and the striped water of Cartagena Bay—layered from indigo to lapis to azure to turquoise like one of my mother's dress designs—were authentic.

In the week, or *ocho días*, as Colombians say, I returned from Cartagena with a completed rough draft.

My writer friend and I opened another bottle of champagne.

Still avoiding a plan, I let another friend persuade me to attend a two-week writers' conference in Boulder where James Dickey would be a featured instructor.

I'd seen Jim once in New Orleans after he became "the famous poet." He gave a reading, and with my UNO colleagues Kenneth and Malcolm, I went to hear him. By that time he no longer mentioned his Phi Beta Kappa key and he'd nurtured a Southern hick accent, often stopping in midstanza to marvel, "Ain't that a great line?"

After the reading, we stood in the hall while Jim left with Miller Williams, and as they passed, Jim put his hands on my shoulders, leaned down, and kissed me on the lips.

Malcolm gasped. "What nerve!"

I didn't try to explain that it was the only time Jim had ever kissed me.

In Boulder, when my friend and I entered the conference center, she spotted Jim in a wing chair surrounded by young females. "Oh, look! There's the great man himself."

Jim glanced up just then and sprang from the chair. "Pat!"

He stepped around the girls and enfolded me in a great bear hug.

He kept me beside him all evening, telling me how much he resented Rice ("McKillop didn't want me around unless I became a reputable scholar. He kept insisting on that goddamned Ph.D. He didn't care how much time I'd lost in the war."), and the next day when I went to his class, my friend said I had to move from the first row.

"He talks only to you. When you're in the front, he never looks away from you. You spoil the session for everyone else."

Jim begged me to stick with him until his girl arrived the following weekend—a girl he coyly called "Miss Hannah," who wasn't the wife Maxine I knew from Rice—so he could fend off the female poets who wanted to sleep with him. He took me along to the Boulder faculty cocktail parties and wine and cheese evenings so he could have me on his arm. Because, of course, sex was part of what writing conferences were apparently all about. The women poets there *did* want to sleep with Jim and be discovered, and both the conferees and the directors seemed to expect a sort of de rigueur "adventure" during their two weeks away from home.

Jim and I also occasionally went out to dinner with another attendee, a young playwright named Will Simms, and with the other conference instructor/writers Nelson Algren and Charlotte and Maurice Zolotov.

Charlotte, who wrote children's books and probably knew how "literary" writers devalued them, kept quiet. Maurice had just finished a biography of Marilyn Monroe, and while his dinner conversation centered on what a voracious sexual appetite Marilyn had, I thought her behavior sounded more and more pitiful. She became more a needy child than the vixen he thought he was portraying, and although I didn't interrupt him, I wanted to defend her. Algren spent his evenings moaning that he'd sold his one blockbuster novel outright for five thousand dollars. "Would you believe? Five thousand lousy bucks."

I wanted to remind him that his name was still on the book and on the film and that the whole world knew he'd written *The Man with the Golden Arm*.

But of course I didn't say anything.

By 1968 Dickey had packed on too much weight to play the trim, muscular athlete any longer, but he continued to extol his prowess as a football star, his status on the college track team. He added new heroics from the wars Dr. McKillop wouldn't give him academic credit for, and while he was no Lieutenant Faversham, he was convincing enough that I didn't realize until years later, when I read Henry Hart's biography of him, just how many facts he'd invented.

I don't remember if I'd detected Dickey's sexual ambivalence back at Rice, but in Colorado, I often caught him eyeing young male poets. Once when we sat alone at lunch, he stared openly at a tanned matinee-idol type before he finally confessed, "You know, if I'm ever tempted by a male, that would be the kind of boy I could go for."

I assumed he felt safe murmuring that to me since I stood as a buffer to the omnivorous females he wanted to avoid. And when a pretty young poet, Jane, went with me to his dorm room to hear him play ragged guitar, I could tell that he envisioned himself a romantic—and Byronic— mentor to us both. With me there, he could safely flirt with Jane in his overbearing way and still avoid taking her to bed.

One morning after class she and I walked from campus into town and as we passed a silver shop, she pointed to a bulky silver ring with an Indian motif. "Doesn't that look like Dickey? Why don't we pool our money and buy it for him?"

In Hart's *James Dickey*, I wasn't surprised to see a 1985 photo of Jim wearing a bulky sterling ring with a heavy Indian design.

Next to James Dickey, the most famous instructor at the conference was Robert Gover, author of the mega best seller *One Hundred Dollar Misunderstanding.* Even though I could tell at the first class that he was no teacher and that he didn't have anything significant to say about writing, he did have compelling blue eyes behind horn-rimmed glasses, and his critiques were kind. So I went to his sessions.

I also listened to him, and within a couple of days we were eating together at a cafeteria table the other conferees called "the power table," or we went to lunch with Dickey, Hannah, and Will Simms or out to dinner alone. Once a group of us escaped to Cheyenne in Gover's rented car and attended the kind of hot, dry, and amateurish rodeo I'd gone to as a kid. The bronc riders fell off within three seconds and the bulls tossed their cowboys before they left the gate while we sat in the bleachers and wiped dust from our sweaty faces. Jim yawned, but Bob said endearingly, "Well, the horses are pretty."

I also spent a lot of time with Will. Although possibly a decade or so younger than I was, he was one of the sharpest writers at the conference. He'd written a couple of brilliant one-acts and TV scripts, and I later learned he also played spectacular poker.

On the evening Jim was scheduled to read, I filed into the auditorium with other conference-goers and Boulder college students, and I saw Will at the end of a row with an empty seat beside him. I stopped and looked down. "I've got three kids, but if you let me have that empty seat, I'll give you the remaining fourth of my love."

He gazed up while he scooted over. "You can't give me a quarter of your love, Pat. Love is indivisible. If you give me any of it, you have to give me all."

Jim worked hard those two weeks to impress me with his success. He hinted that he'd won both the National Book Award and the Pulitzer Prize, and once he said, "Would you believe I had to pay sixteen thousand dollars in income tax last year alone?"

A few days later when I asked Bob if he'd owed that much tax, he gave a small smile. "I paid a lot more than that, Pat." (Not until years later did I realize Jim's mythical sixteen-thousand-dollar tax bill had been the salary he'd been offered for a teaching job.)

I'd come to the conference to avoid thinking, and Jim and I often walked across campus discussing Rice and the 1968 presidential race, and he kept trying to convince me that the fine poet—and his dearest friend—Eugene McCarthy (whose close friendship I recognized, like Faulkner's, was a stretch) would win the primary and the election.

"Come on, Jim. He hasn't got a prayer."

"Just wait. You'll see. He's going to be elected."

He'd always been too beefy—and always a bit too naïve—for me, but abruptly, under that Colorado sky, I realized how much he wanted me to believe in his wisdom.

And if I'd assumed his Pygmalion role back in our Rice days had been partially a figment of my own imagination, I recognized at the Boulder conference that he as well had imagined himself in the Svengali part. That was especially clear the evening he signed his poetry collection to me with the dedication, "To Pat Moore Esslinger—who, by being who she is and who she has become, vindicates me."

At the end of the conference, Jim with his usual directness asked, "What's wrong with that boy you're married to? You interested in that young playwright?"

Since Jim was also an alcoholic, I ignored the first question and sidestepped the second with, "I think I'm interested in Bob. He's a Scorpio, and they're my weakness."

He frowned. "You two going to get together?"

I'd already debated whether Bob would do for an affair, and I shrugged. "When school starts, I asked if he wanted to come to New Orleans to talk to my fiction class."

I hadn't made future plans yet, and I'd be teaching at UNO that fall, so when Bob called from Malibu, we firmed up his lecture.

But the second I saw him gliding up the airport escalator in New Orleans, I could tell he'd assumed that the invitation meant we were going to become lovers.

He pulled me into a passionate kiss, and when I finally backed away I said, "You'll like this. The parents of the kids in my class realized your book had sex scenes between a black prostitute and a white college kid, so they rushed to the bookstore and bought every copy. I had to reorder to give the students a chance to read the book."

"They bought every copy!" He threw back his head and laughed before he kissed me again. "If I'd known you before, I'd have been a real best-selling author. You're the most beautiful woman in the world."

"No, actually, I'm an ugly woman. I just know what I'm doing."

His hands tightened on my shoulders and he stared for a long moment into my face. "Well then, you're the most beautiful ugly woman I've ever seen."

Bob spoke to the students, who were thrilled by his humility, his leather biker's jacket, and the shades he wore indoors. He, of course, despised the Vietnam War, he advocated recreational drugs, and his answers to social questions were predictable for 1968, but when one student asked him to name his favorite authors, he glanced at me and smiled. "Besides your professor, that is?"

I don't think he'd read anything I'd written, but it was a charming compliment, and I accepted it as another of his endearing qualities.

After the class I ferried him across Lake Pontchartrain for a party arranged so he could meet Walker Percy.

Percy had expressed his admiration for Bob's *The Maniac Responsible*, and the minute we got there, the host introduced the two famous authors to each other.

They must have spoken a sentence each—Percy probably repeating his admiration, and Bob probably saying something equally pleasant about *The Moviegoer*—before they drifted in opposite directions, looking uncomfortable and harried.

I didn't see them say a word to each other again.

After perhaps an hour, Percy made his escape, and the hostess took pity on Bob and handed him a camcorder so he could stand apart and film without having to make conversation with the other guests.

He almost relaxed as he hovered silently around the edge of the crowd, but I'm not sure he actually took a deep breath until we were driving the thirty miles back across the lake to his hotel.

The next night Kenneth and I took Bob to a student party.

A bowl of Black Beauties and Quaaludes sat on the coffee table, and I knew at once that this kind of drug and keg bash was more his milieu.

He let me introduce him around, and while we circulated, he made comments to the students about the war and the pigs and how we all needed to organize, sit in or drop out, and rescue the country from Johnson's war.

For a first affair, I'd hoped for a little more depth and originality, but I told myself that since he didn't know the students, he was undoubtedly giving them what he thought they wanted to hear. Since I'd never been able to tell what Scorpios really thought (probably the reason they fascinated me), I told myself he wasn't actually as conventional as he sounded.

But as the evening lurched toward midnight and he began tossing back Black Beauties as if they'd been party peanuts, I realized that he wasn't the right replacement for Jack after all. So I relinquished him to a student, Genelle, who accompanied him back to the Hotel de Ville.

In the morning when I went by the Quarter to take him to the airport, Genelle waved a radiant good-bye. "I'll see you in Malibu in a couple of weeks, Bob."

"She thinks I'm going to marry her," he said as I drove down Airline. "But there's only one person I would marry right now in case you're interested."

It wasn't quite the time to say I no longer was.

I started something at UNO when I arranged to have Bob talk to my class, and pretty soon, famous authors were filing through the halls, including Shirley Ann Grau, who'd just won the Pulitzer Prize, Ralph Ellison, and William Styron.

I'd known a woman in Cali whose brother had brought Styron home for the holidays during their college years. "He was the biggest pain. He told us he was going to be rich and famous, so he just sat on the couch and ordered snacks and drinks. Before the term started and my brother took him back to school, we were sick to the teeth of him."

He wasn't particularly a pain to our UNO students, and only by accident had he ruined one grad student's master's work on *Lie Down in Darkness* by saying that the German phrase on which the boy's whole thesis hinged was actually a misprint. But he couldn't have treated our colleague Cynthia more shabbily.

After his talk, he called loud attention to the fact that he was going home to sleep with her, and as I watched him I wondered if he needed to create for us, or perhaps himself, a myth of sexual prowess.

Cynthia didn't seem to care which it was, and the next morning she floated down the hall proudly displaying a greasy brown paper bag—the kind in which French Quarter shops wrap muffaletta sandwiches—with his signature. She blissfully told everyone he'd invited her to New York. "He's going to call when he gets a date set up. I might even give up this crummy job and stay in New York with him."

Of course, he never called.

One evening, when Jack drove by to pick up the children from my friend Leona's, he was so drunk she refused to let the kids climb in the car with him. She called me, and after I got out of class, she came to the house with us to see if Jack was all right.

He wasn't home.

"He was pretty sloshed," she said. "Let's drive around the neighborhood."

I'd seen how completely blind drunk he became on a single whiskey sour, and I didn't know why I hadn't suspected before, but that night, I discovered a shabby bar a dozen blocks from our house, tucked into a row of shops beside a dingy grocery.

I stopped the car and Leona and I went in. "Did anyone here happen to see a young man in a pin-striped suit with a briefcase?"

"Oh, you mean Jack?" The bartender swiped a rag across the bar. "He comes in every night about five, stays for an hour or so. He was here, but he's already gone."

I had assumed six o'clock was the time he got off the Freret bus and walked home.

We called the police, and an officer came by, but before we'd finished describing Jack, he looked up and closed his notebook. "So that's who he is. A physician pulled him over and made a citizen's arrest a couple of hours ago. He's at the Canal Street Lockup."

Jack sat on a metal bench in an anteroom made of two sets of bars, separated from both the cells and the drunk tank but nonetheless surrounded by the station's overwhelming stench of urine. As he saw me, he mumbled, "Why did that busybody doctor have to interfere with me? Why couldn't he mind his own business?"

I was signing the release papers, and I didn't have to answer.

New Orleans was a party town, so until the semester ended, I continued to give elegant—albeit frugal—parties at which I served batter-fried cubes of guinea pig (passed off as "squirrel") on sterling plates. At an evening for Jack's parasitology class, a new first-year resident helped me pass the homemade dips and crackers. He was one of those extremely attractive students also interested in literature, so as the party wound down, we sat in the library and talked about books.

"Have you read Malcolm Lowry's *Under the Volcano?*"

I confessed I hadn't.

"I have a copy in my apartment. I can drop it by if you want me to."

"I'd like that."

He came by with the novel a week later, and I might have offered him a goblet of wine if I hadn't had an evening class. As it was, I didn't see him again until after I'd finished Lowry's story of the hopeless alcoholic who dies in a trench beside the pariah dogs.

That was a few days after I'd brought the children home from school to find Jack curled in a drunken stupor in the front hall. Five-year-old Sean looked down at him on the hardwood floor. "Poor Daddy. He gets so tired."

I could tell he was trying to excuse Jack, and I decided no little boy should have to do that.

And of course I knew why Jack's student had suggested I read *Under the Volcano*.

One of the last big parties I gave in New Orleans was
a Christmas open house that included most of the medical
school faculty and their children. I made little Christmas
tree piñatas filled with chocolates and a tiny toy for the
kids, a sterling punch bowl filled with whiskey sours and
floating orange slices for the adults. My father had flown
over from Houston for the holidays, and as I watched him
sitting beside Dr. Smith from surgery, I realized that he was
actually talking to her. He drank one bourbon all evening.

I stood between my bulb-lit tree and the oak table and
thought how sad it was that my father hadn't attended
college. I knew Dr. Smith had gone to medical school in
Heidelberg just as Hitler came to power, and I wished I
could tell her that my little Irish father would have known
all about the era they'd lived through. I wished I could tell
her he'd make a great dinner companion even though he
wasn't a professional, that he'd read all of Shakespeare, including *Coriolanus*, and he knew politics and ancient history.

He once told me that when he'd gone to work for Standard Oil, the Grass Creek boss at the time had said they
didn't need any office help unless he knew how to type and
take shorthand. "Can you do that?"

He said he learned to type over the weekend and that
he made up his own shorthand system by the end of the
first week.

I glanced at him beside Dr. Smith and I wanted to tell
her all of that.

But naturally I didn't say anything.

I didn't know anyone who'd left a marriage without another prospect waiting in the wings, but since that wasn't my case, and since I knew if I decided on a divorce I'd have to support myself and three children, I asked the head of the UNO English Department for a full-time job.

He looked at me sympathetically. "There are just too many Tulane Ph.D.s on the staff, Pat. (He didn't say "male Ph.D.s," but I could hear the echo of it.) I can let you have a permanent part-time position, but I don't think you'll ever be hired full time."

That meant I'd have to leave New Orleans. But since I wouldn't be able to find an academic job in the middle of the year, I had to stay at UNO through the spring semester.

So I flew to Malibu to see if I'd made a mistake by letting Bob go. He was laid-back, obviously attracted to me, and even if he was currently writing sequels and naïvely Brechtian plays, he *had* made a million dollars on his one best seller.

But when we arrived at his beach house and he immediately passed around a joint, I had to accept that he was as ordinary as I'd hoped he wasn't.

He inhaled and pointed to a huge black rock rising from the ocean. "Look at that thing. How could anyone write good stuff here? I think I'll go to Majorca for a year."

Writing in Majorca smacked of the same cliché as Malibu, that stereotypical flight from civilization toward creativity wealthy authors could afford to make, but I didn't say that, and although he may have waited for me to tell him I'd like to escape with him, I didn't say that either.

When I left Malibu, Bob said, "I'll write and let you know how Genelle and I are doing."

The cards and phone calls—one of which informed me that Genelle had had a baby ("A boy! I'm going to name him Bryan.")—were infrequent, and it turned out that he couldn't write in Majorca either.

Then a collect call came from the Tombs in New York.

"We've been arrested for possession. We had a couple of pounds of hash hidden in the diaper bag. But, you know, I think the experience could give me something to write about. I'm calling to see if you'll take Bryan for a couple of years while we go to jail."

"Genelle agrees to that?"

"We both saw you with your kids. We know what a great mother you are."

"Of course I'll take him."

"I knew you would."

"But there's a catch, Bob. I won't give him back."

"What?"

"Give me iron-clad adoption papers, and I'll take him. But I'm not giving all my love to a baby and then tearing out a chunk of my heart to let him go again."

I heard in the silence that he knew I meant it, and when he hung up, I didn't hear from him for another month until he called to say that the drug charge had been dropped. "It turns out if you spend enough on lawyers, you can get off."

"I always suspected as much."

That spring I gave a series of farewell dinners, at the last of which Jack became too drunk to talk before I'd served the chicken Kiev.

I steered him to the bedroom and went back to the dinner guests. "He had a flu shot this afternoon. I guess that first martini knocked him out completely."

Since they all came from the medical school, I could tell they knew better, and the next morning, one of the wives called. "Ken told me to tell you that you're a real lady."

A week later she called again to say that she was selling Ken's chair. "I know you like it, and I wondered if you wanted to buy it."

When I'd seen the ladder-back with the rush seat at their house and had admired it, Ken told me it had been made in 1595 and had sat by the hearth in his family's home in Edinburgh for all those centuries. ("Shakespeare could have used it for all I know.") I knew how much he valued it, and I suspected his wife was selling it because she'd found out—as I had when I'd lived in Cali—that he was having his own Colombian adventure, an affair with a young, dyed-blond secretary at the Valle del Cauca Medical School, whenever he made trips to South America.

"I'm asking $125 for it if you want it."

I suppose at that moment I realized I was more my sister's keeper than my brother's, and I said, "Are you sure you don't want to put the price higher? It's worth a great deal more than $125."

"I'll ask more if I sell it to someone else."

"In that case, I'll be right over to get it."

I'd read about the harm that could come to children from divorce. And 1969 wasn't that far from the 1930s when a divorced woman became almost an untouchable. Few faculty wives I knew were divorcées, I couldn't think of anyone at UNO who was divorced, and while my grandmothers apparently had divorced their husbands, they were both dead. And I didn't have anyone to talk to. Would my kids be teased unmercifully in their elementary school classes? Or maybe shunned by their classmates? How would the three of them feel having a single working mother?

But I also suspected that living with a serious alcoholic might be more harmful, and I wondered if having a series of affairs could make up for what I didn't have with Jack. Perhaps I could keep the marriage intact if I went my own way and picked my own lovers. And affairs—like jail for Bob—might give me something else to write about.

So that same spring, I sampled that.

But just as Bob had been too conventional, Ronnie was too young, and Rich too dangerous.

One of my female colleagues stopped me in the hall and murmured, "You have to have a death wish to sleep with that guy. I think he's a sociopath."

I shook my head. "He admits to being a sociopath. Defining it his way, anyone who doesn't conform is a sociopath. My guess is he's a full-blown psychopath."

Another of my guesses was that affairs weren't the answer.

And I realized without actually articulating it that I shouldn't stay for the sake of the children. I should leave for their sake.

So I didn't go again to Malibu. Nor did I go to New York.

I went instead to teach at the University of Texas in El Paso, commonly called UTEP.

My sister Honey's army major husband had just returned from Vietnam and was stationed at Fort Bliss, and she'd enrolled in grad school. One day in the spring, she phoned. "Pat, I heard there's an opening in the department. Why don't you come here?"

I called the English department chair, John West.

"Yes, I know who you are. Your sister just talked to me. But from what she says, you're too good for this place. Why would you want to teach at this school?"

"I'm getting a divorce."

I could hear him nod. "Well, divorcées should stick together. I'm in a divorce myself. But let me warn you, you can't cross the border and get a quick one any longer."

"That's all right. I want a legal one anyway."

He paused a second. "I can offer you only ten thousand dollars."

"I'll take it."

I sent the children by plane to Honey's while I packed everything I could—including my Colombian emerald green wool ruana and my favorite pre-Columbian artifacts—into my red Fiat and drove 1,208 miles across Louisiana and Texas. As I drove, I worried. I'd earned the respect of New Orleans' students, but what if I alienated those with a rich border culture?

But as I paused on the final hill and saw the yellow lights of El Paso, suddenly I felt as if I were coming home.

I'd arrived in El Paso, but I still hesitated to start divorce proceedings.

Possibly my leaving would jar Jack at last into miraculous recovery—or at least into AA—and he'd do a heroic act that would allow me to avoid a final split. I'd waited for him to change; perhaps I could wait longer. Or possibly the whole idea of severing a fourteen-year relationship gave me the nausea of losing an arm. And in El Paso as I bought four beds, a table and four chairs, and three graduated cubes as pedestals for my three best pre-Columbian pieces, I consoled myself that I was "separated," not divorced.

The children voted and commissioned me to paint the secondhand furniture bright red—a garish and glossy vermilion to cheer up a dun-colored desert town. So on our third night in El Paso as the wind bellied the glass of the kitchen window, loosened the putty, and lashed dry yucca pods across the window-framed sky, I painted the table and chairs on spread-out sections of *The El Paso Times.*

The kids had gone to bed, the radio played softly, and as I applied the red-tipped brush, a news flash came on that Sharon Tate and a number of her guests had been brutally murdered at her mansion. The newscaster described how the victims had sustained multiple stab wounds and how they lay on the grass around the estate. "The police said they all looked like they were wearing red clothes."

The kitchen table, which I'd completed, dried on the classifieds while I layered a paint-chipped chair with crimson enamel on the sports page. As it stood half-finished on the newspaper, its scarlet legs and feet glistened in the kitchen overhead light as if it had walked across the bloody lawn of the Tate mansion.

While the wind swirled sand drifts onto the porch tiles of my rented house, I kept dialing Jack's New Orleans number, perhaps wanting to hear a sentence that could save the marriage, perhaps wanting to say the magic words that could save it.

All I got, however, was a $356 phone bill for my first month in El Paso.

Since my take-home pay from the university amounted to $540, and the rent on the house was $150, I had to make an arrangement with the phone company to pay in increments while the four of us lived on macaroni and cheese and lettuce salads.

But El Paso—and Fort Bliss, the size of Rhode Island— harbored hundreds of single men, and I was asked out constantly. Wherever my date took me for dinner, I always ordered a steak. I'd eat a few bites and at the end of the meal ask for a doggie bag so I could take the rest home, cube the beef, and make Irish stew.

The kids ate a lot of that, too.

Unfortunately, the other thing that occurred my first month was that the checks I'd written on mine and Jack's joint New Orleans account for the thrift store furniture, the initial month's rent on the house, and the down payment on a washer, all bounced. I had to go into the English departmental office and explain to my new employer, John West, that I really wasn't some deadbeat trying to rook El Paso merchants.

He always wore cowboy boots—which my mother would have loved—and he always took them off and stood them at the side of his chair. As I finished my explanation, he came around the desk in his usual pair of thick blue socks, reached out, and took my hand. "That kind of thing could happen to any of us in a divorce," he said.

Honey had found me the rent house just beyond Fort Bliss, close to an elementary school, and I'd been in it for a month when I got a call from my New Orleans student, Ronnie, whose curling black hair, black beard, and stained-glass blue eyes had the look—even at nineteen—of a Shakespearean actor. He wanted to come for a visit and talk me into going to Woodstock with him.

"I'm not up for camping or rock music and grass just now, but I am coming back to retrieve some items from Jack's house." I told him he could drive the U-Haul to El Paso for me. "You can stay a week and I'll get you a plane ticket to fly home."

I retraced the 1,208 miles, rented a van, and Ronnie and Jack loaded the truck with my favorite antiques, books, clothes, Ken's chair, a few more pre-Columbian artifacts from the cache I'd collected, a box of shoes—which had molded while I'd been in El Paso—and a carton of wine glasses. Jack's lab assistant had moved in with him, and when she told me how much she loved my watercolors of exotic Colombian fruit, I left those on the wall.

Ronnie and I caravanned back to El Paso.

When we got there, he gazed adoringly at me and played ball with the kids on the withered lawn until finally I told him it was time for him to leave. "You have to find someone your own age. I'm too old for you."

"I'll never find someone thirty-seven who's nineteen. Please let me stay. Marry me, adopt me, hire me. Just let me stay."

It was such a great line that I let him stay for another week.

John West stopped me in the hall. "I want you to teach a graduate class in Faulkner." Walter Taylor had received some kind of research grant from the university so he could revise his Faulkner dissertation into a book, and since no one else was a Faulkner scholar, John added, "I'm giving you the class."

"I'm not a Faulkner scholar either. I've only read two of his novels."

"I can tell you're a quick study."

I was under no illusions. I'd already noticed that the men in the department guarded their territory, and I immediately decided Walter and John had concluded that some woman with an Irish lit specialty, who didn't know Faulkner well and who'd been assigned the graduate course the weekend before school started, would be no threat.

So when I went into class, I had to tell the assembled students that we were all equal and that we'd analyze Faulkner's work together. "Nothing's out of bounds if it's in the text. Just keep in mind, of course, that I'm more equal than the rest of you."

One student dropped the class, but by the second month, the ones who stayed were having such fun discovering unconventional themes no critic had seen that they persuaded me to keep the three-hour seminar and add a Sunday afternoon at my house so they could discuss the novels more at length ("We'll bring the wine, Dr. Esslinger.").

When they—we—came up with a radically new theory showing how Faulkner layered images and characters from comic strips onto his narratives, *Modern Fiction Studies* took the paper, "No Spinach in *Sanctuary*," without hesitation, and Walter murmured wistfully, "I wish just once I'd had a class like that one."

Bea Parker, author's mother, 1920s.

Bea Moore, author's mother in
Grass Creek, Wyoming, 1925.

Stanley Moore, author's father, 1925.

Mike and Pat
Moore, author
and her brother,
1932.

Pat Moore, 1933.

Pat and Mike Moore in front of
their house, 1934.

Pat Moore, 1936.

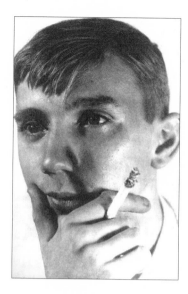

Jack Esslinger, author's
first husband, 1956.
Courtesy of Sean Esslinger.

Duane and Pat
Carr in El Paso,
Texas, 1971.

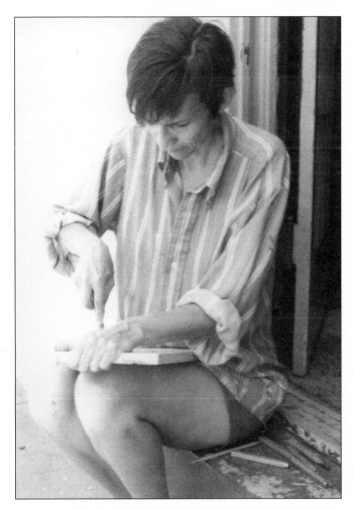

Pat Carr in El Paso, 1976.

Duane and Pat Carr with Jennifer, Shelley, Sean, and Stephanie in Oklahoma visiting the children's grandfather, Cecil Esslinger, 1975.

Pat Carr in Elkins, Arkansas, 1984.

Pat Carr at the International Women's Writing Guild
Conference at Skidmore College, Saratoga Springs,
New York, 1986. *Courtesy of Diane Gallo.*

Pat Carr with Faulkner
and Behn in Elkins,
Arkansas, 1987.
Courtesy of Amy Wilson.

Pat and Duane
Car in Bowling
Green, Kentucky,
1990.

The South and West Literature Conference was held that year in Pine Bluff, Arkansas, and since I'd just won their short fiction award, I got an invitation to speak about short stories.

I hadn't been full-time faculty long enough to know I might get the university to pay transportation costs, so I left the children with Honey and scraped together enough of my own money to fly from El Paso to the tiny airport in Pine Bluff.

No one was there to meet me, and after waiting an hour, I went to the information desk. "Would you please call me a taxi? I need to get into town."

The girl behind the counter stared. "A taxi?"

A man passing the counter stopped and pushed his Caterpillar cap back on his forehead. "I have a pickup outside. I can take you into town if you want me to."

"That would be great."

As he drove, he asked what I was doing in Pine Bluff, and I told him about the three-day conference and my speech, "The Death of the Short Story." "I'm basically saying that if authors keep writing cynical literature, if they don't believe in love or make readers care about their characters, then fiction, particularly short stories, are dead."

He nodded, we reached the conference center, and I thanked him for the ride.

The next afternoon, I got a call in my motel room from him. "I came to your lecture last night, and I'd like to see you again. Could I take you to dinner?"

My life was already too complicated. I couldn't add Pine Bluff, Arkansas, and I had to tell him "No, thank you." But I felt really bad about saying it.

By the time I left New Orleans, I'd had a third story, "Desire Is a Bus," accepted by *Phylon* and a chapbook, *From Beneath the Hill,* in press. I'd won the South and West Fiction Award and a Library of Congress Marc IV Award, and I had critical articles in *Modern Drama, Western Humanities Review,* and *Books Abroad.* So although the stories had the wrong point of view, I set out for El Paso in a flush of publishing success.

I'd also taught in college for a decade, and when I asked a black male and a white girl to do a staged reading of Leroi Jones's *Dutchman* in my freshman communication class, I intended to illustrate its theme that violence results when words fail.

But that September, words had already failed between Vietnam War supporters and antiwar protesters, and many veterans who came back from their time "in country" to take classes at UTEP were undeniably suspicious of a teacher wearing an ankh (a modernistic one with a centered glass blue eye that Gover had given me) on a thong.

The afternoon after the reading, John West and the dean of humanities called me into John's office. They sat together behind the desk, waiting with grim faces. "We've heard complaints about your class. Why did you assign that play?"

Their shoulder-to-shoulder intimidation attempt was unmistakable, and I wondered whose idea it had been as I glanced at John's free-standing cowboy boots and asked, "Have you read the play?"

They stared at me in silence for a moment before they shook their heads.

"I'll put copies in your boxes."

A week later I got the plays back. Neither of them mentioned *Dutchman* again.

Wary of more bouncing checks, I cleaned out the New Orleans savings account. It didn't contain much money, but since Jack had dropped the children from his medical school health plan, I rationalized that I could use the savings for an emergency.

And I could use a few dollars to purchase the ancient Mimbres pottery I'd accidentally stumbled across in a run-down filling station at the edge of the desert.

I spotted the bowls and guessed they were authentic the second I saw them under the dusty glass of the counter. Black and white Mimbres Classic, coiled, painted, fired by ancient pueblo dwellers between 800 and 1000 A.D., they all belonged in a museum.

My breath faltered and my palms began to sweat. "Could I look at those?"

The craggy proprietor reached in, lifted them out, and put them on the counter.

Each bowl had splintered into dozens of pieces in the "kill" that smashed it to let the spirit escape the corpse on whose skull it had been placed, and the bowls had been scrupulously glued back together. The second I touched the grainy white slips and iron black designs of a rabbit, dual turkeys, a four-footed carp, I knew the bowls were real.

"Friend a mine digs them up with a backhoe." The old man watched me, gauging what I'd pay. "I can let you have them cheap."

A backhoe would destroy 50 percent of the bowls in any burial site and 100 percent of the archaeological data. But these bowls would disappear if I left them. Someone who didn't know what they were might even crack them apart again and scatter them with gravel on a garden path.

So once again, I expanded the market.

It was a Cloudcroft picnic, designed to check October aspens, given for single faculty and graduate students, and one of the kids on a far blanket was the green-eyed, first-year graduate student, Duane Carr, who'd sat through the first day of my Faulkner seminar, made a few bright comments, then dropped the course.

After the fried chicken and brownies, everyone dutifully prepared for the hike to view the aspen leaves. But not in a hiking mood, I resisted all urging, even offers of loaned tennis shoes to replace my sandals, and the other picnickers finally filed off.

The one person left was the good-looking graduate student, who picked up a liter of burgundy and two paper cups and came over to my blanket. "I heard you were a writer. I've always wanted to be a writer myself."

Since he was too young for me, I said crisply, "A writer is someone who writes."

But he didn't seem put off, and as he poured us wine he said, "I also overheard you say you'd flown to Colombia to write a book. What are you doing at this university?"

"I'm separated. It seemed far enough away."

"You have kids?"

Strangely enough for a male, he asked additional questions ("How old?" "Are they with you?") and listened to my answers. We kept talking until the others returned.

When everyone piled into the cars and stopped at the Red Dog Saloon in Cloudcroft, however, and he sat at a table with one of my older female colleagues, I saw that he was basically just a polite kid.

But he certainly had hypnotic, listening eyes.

John West had decided UTEP needed a course in black literature, and even though I usually joked that he offered me the class because I had the darkest tan in the department, I *had* taught African American lit. So I accepted the class, and when my young office mate, Tom Green, asked if I'd like to write a paper with him, defining the differences between white and black authors, I agreed to that, too.

Tom, with a master's in folklore, hypothesized that white writers focused on achieving, but that black writers wrote characters who merely existed. To test the theory, we set up a content analysis study to look at stories by a score of white males—Hemingway, Steinbeck, Bellow, Roth, Updike—and a score by black males—Wright, Ellison, Hughes, Gaines, and others. As we analyzed, we saw that white characters always worked toward a goal. (In Anderson's "Death in the Woods," "things had to be fed. Men had to be fed, and the horses . . . the poor thin cow . . . Horses, cows, pigs, dogs, men.") The black writers used protagonists like Mann in "Down by the Riverside" who in a flood leaned against a damp wall and did nothing. ("He should have cleared out when the Government offered him the boat. Now he had no money for a boat.") He had no goal, no gleam of success. He just waited and hoped to survive.

It was Tom's premise, and I thought it brilliant. But it was the first paper I'd tried to write with a male, and I recognized right away the flaw in Jung's myth of men's superior organizational skills. I spent most of my time trying to keep Tom on the theme.

Nonetheless we finished the article, and when we submitted it, *Afro-American Forum* took it at once.

Researching black literature, I'd tried to examine every aspect of slavery. So in the El Paso flea market, I had no trouble identifying the dusty slave mask marked $1.50. Used to punish slaves without losing their field labor, it had four iron bands that hugged the skull and locked the face and neck into an iron collar. Welded to the center band was a biscuit-sized nosepiece with air holes and four prongs to press down the tongue. The iron prongs kept the slave from swallowing his own saliva, and after a day in the sun, the nosepiece often cooked his nose into a slab of baked meat.

I took it to class to educate students too young to know antebellum history, but most of my colleagues shuddered and said, "That's horrible! Why remind students of such an ugly past?" I resisted the idea of stifling any knowledge, but I gave up trying to convince them that some events shouldn't be forgotten, and a few years later, I was persuaded to give it to Dorothy Redford when she came to campus to give a reading.

I'd met her and had read her *Somerset Homecoming* that documented how a plantation reunion brought together descendants of her slave family, the overseers, and owners, and I knew she was to be curator of the museum at the North Carolina plantation. So I brought the mask in a brown paper bag and handed it to her. "For the museum."

My colleagues held their collective breath and waited while she opened the bag and took out the gruesome iron bands and iron collar.

She stared at it a moment before she looked up. "What a great example of the resilience of the human spirit! To put someone in this, and have him come out still a human being, is really a testament to the goodness of mankind, isn't it?"

One afternoon in the English office, John introduced me to a beautiful black graduate student from the History Department who taught classes at Fort Bliss. "Nona wants you to come to her class one of these evenings and talk about black literature," John said.

Nona studied me and when John left, she said, "You're not black, are you?"

I shook my head. "But I once passed for black—accidentally—at Texas Southern University in Houston."

"Let's go to the Kern Place Tavern and I'll buy you a beer."

I recounted my experience and confessed my white guilt and my inability to improve the students' English in a brief semester. Then I listened to the tragedy of her young husband who'd had such faith in Johnson's Civil Rights Bill that when nothing changed, he held a pistol to his heart and pulled the trigger.

"People imagine committing suicide by putting a gun in their mouths or against their temples, but the surest way is to go for the heart."

She told how she tried to instill black pride in her four-year-old. "I let him find an empty stocking on Christmas morning and I tell him, 'Never count on a stingy old white bastard like Santa.' Then as he starts to cry, I fling open the closet door and say, 'But look here. I got you plenty of presents. You can trust someone who looks like me.'"

She told about her own moment of truth, that realization of her own blackness. "In kindergarten the other kids told me to play the wolf in our game of Red Riding Hood." Her dark eyes looked at me from across the table. "Until that moment, I'd thought of myself as Red Riding Hood."

In the black literature course, which attracted some white students but was mostly an African American class, I taught that slave narratives, sermons, poems, and stories could illustrate the "peculiar institution" and the tragic legacy of slavery, but I also insisted that literature couldn't be just a polemic on the evils of the system. "If literature isn't universal, if it doesn't promote understanding or deal with the human spirit and conflicts of the human heart, it won't last."

Occasionally I'd get an argument ("It's our heritage. Why should it have to appeal to whites, too?" or "You're asking too much of a work, Dr. Esslinger."), but more often I'd hear, as one black Vietnam veteran said, "I agree with you, Doc. Stories got to work for everybody. And, you know, I keep forgetting that we're not all brothers and sisters gathered around this seminar table."

A few nights later I was sitting with Nona, a few of those other brothers and sisters, and a number of black townspeople and black army personnel from Fort Bliss the night Jesse Jackson came to El Paso to speak.

Wearing an afro the size of a small tumbleweed, a huge silver medallion centered on his chest, and a leather vest with matching trousers, he strode back and forth across the stage, telling the students to get a decent education and to achieve. "Black power is worth working for, but it comes with a price. 'Burn, baby, burn' is a catchy slogan, but when you take over the electric plant, you better know how to run it."

Nona nudged me with her elbow.

Jesse and his afro had probably gotten the point across better than I had.

My first Christmas in El Paso, Jack came for the holiday.

I don't know what I'd expected, but it wasn't to have the stewardess help him down the plane's metal stairs or to have him sway drunkenly toward the car with me.

Fortunately, the plane had been the last one into the terminal that night, and the children had already gone to bed before we got to the little house near Fort Bliss.

The next morning Jack seemed sober, and he could talk briefly to the children while they ate breakfast. When they went out to play, he admired the artifacts I'd brought from New Orleans and looked enviously at my recently acquired black and white Mimbres bowls. He'd stayed interested in archaeology after we'd left Colombia, and he was a good student when he wasn't drunk, so he, too, recognized the bowls' authenticity.

He carefully picked up the white-slipped bowl with the black rabbit in the center. "You know these are going to go for hundreds of thousands of dollars one of these days. You could be on easy street."

"And it's a federal offense to sell them. I don't think I want a street that easy."

In the evening, I took him to a faculty party, where he passed out.

On Christmas morning, he didn't make it through opening presents before his eyes blurred and his words became incomprehensible.

By the end of the holiday I knew that whatever my hopes had been, I had to let them—and him—go.

Members of the Political Science Department had incorporated me into their Thank-God-It's-Friday afternoons at the Kern Place Tavern near campus, and early in the spring semester when a couple of them came in with the news that they, too, were leaving marriages, I felt a wave of guilt.

I told myself that the dissolving and restructuring of relationships were simply parts of the Zeitgeist of 1970, but at the same time, even as I stood on the ice floe by myself, I *had* walked away. And I didn't know if my act had influenced them.

So when I got my new car tag, CRY ★ 280—bearing a tiny Texas star between the Y and the 2—I brought it to the tavern. "I thought this was appropriate for what we're going through."

Ed laughed. "Hey, you're the one divorcée around here none of us ever feels sorry for. You make it seem easy."

I looked at him. "It's not easy for any of us."

"Come on. I don't think you ever loved the guy you're getting rid of."

I didn't try to explain about creativity or heroism or about how it feels to have someone repeatedly turn into a vegetable before your very eyes each evening by seven.

Nor did I say that in spite of everything, you still remember walking into a New Orleans lounge beside him as the elegant pianist glances up and starts to play "Moonlight in Vermont" for him.

At noon sun-dried gold light flowed from the horizon to the edges of El Paso's yellow brick downtown buildings and across the yards of the pale yellow adobes on Rim Road. Stiffened ocotillo plants swayed and rattled in the wind, and at sunset the hot dirt hills surrounding the city flattened into the black sameness of construction-paper peaks against a throbbing melon sky. El Paso nights never turned quite black, however, and even at 2:00 a.m. green hues tinted the midnight blue of the almost darkness.

The children and I had arrived in the breathless 104° heat of summer, but since desert seasons change imperceptibly, we'd been a few weeks into autumn before I realized that the only way El Pasoans could tell when summer had eased into fall was to make that drive to Cloudcroft in the New Mexico mountains to see if the aspen leaves had turned gold and if the piñon cones had burst open to resin-coated nuts.

The fall days stayed hot and the college classrooms stayed air-conditioned until suddenly one afternoon the absolutely clear sky was abruptly, between one class bell and the next, spread with gray cloud cover, and bits of white, more like large dust motes than flakes, began to waver down as if from building roofs rather than the sky, and we knew it was winter.

Spring, of course, was recognizable only by the fact that the cactus pads growing wild at intersections on Mesa blossomed into crumpled yellow tissue paper flowers that could have been *hecho en México*.

"Did I tell you I work for the Mafia?" Joe ordered us a couple of beers.

He was on his third try at freshman English, and I knew he wouldn't have brought up anything personal if the political scientists had gathered. But it was early afternoon, and just the two of us sat at the tavern table, so he added, "I train greyhounds for the Juarez races. You want to go with me and see the dogs run one a these days?"

I stalled. "I didn't know the mob was into greyhound racing."

"Oh, yeah. The boss loves dogs." He glanced over his stein and white beer foam. "You know, the head of the West Coast operation is coming through in a couple a weeks. He don't get to meet dames with class. Just bimbos and floozies. How about when he comes, I give you a call? You and him can go to dinner."

"Just what I need. A blind date from the Mafia."

"Hey, he ain't some mug off the street. He's got a degree from Harvard. And he's got connections. He could get you published just like that."

"A sort of 'who you know' with a death wish."

"What?"

"With three kids in tow, I don't need to get mixed up with the Mafia."

A couple of weeks later he nonetheless called with word that the West Coast head had arrived in town. When I repeated "No, thanks," he said, "It's just a dinner date. I think you and him will hit it off."

"Joe, that's exactly what I'm afraid of."

John West was going to marry a student, Lucy, in the spring: his second marriage and her first. But since she still lived at home and had a wedding to plan, he couldn't see her often, so he took me to basketball games or dropped by my house with a bottle of rum. "It's good in tea with sugar. You know how to make a cup of tea?"

"I know how to make a cup of tea."

He followed me into the kitchen and fondled the back of my neck. "We're both single. We're both lonely. I don't see why we shouldn't get together if we feel like it. It's an affair that won't hurt anyone, and it'll end as soon as I get married."

That sounded so logical. I leaned into his hand and turned off the tea kettle.

I hadn't planned on his appearing three or four times a week. I hadn't realized he'd park his car down the block and monitor every man who entered my house. Nor had I planned on his saying one evening, "Lucy told me that if I meet someone who loves me as much as she does, she'll let me go."

I cared about him, but I couldn't say what he wanted to hear, and I fumbled. "For her to love you that much— For her to make such an offer— What a wonderful girl!"

The whole department was invited to the wedding, and as I went through the receiving line and whispered to him, "Good-bye, John," I knew I'd miss him.

A month or so after Joe confessed his Mafia connection and invited me to dinner with the West Coast boss, he came to my little adobe house with a bottle of tequila. "I got a proposition for you. I need a driver and I thought of you. It pays five thousand dollars."

"Five thousand dollars! That's half my year's salary."

He nodded. "I thought you could use the cash."

"You want me to drive across Texas and then north to Nova Scotia?"

"Naw. It's four, five miles."

"And that pays five thousand dollars?"

He nodded again. "You're the one person I know with the class and composure so border guards don't give you a cross-eyed look. You take a taxi to the Pronof in Juarez, pick up a Cadillac in the *mercado* parking lot, drive back across the bridge, and breeze through customs. Piece of cake."

"I see. And what's in the Cadillac that's worth five thousand dollars?"

He shrugged. "Who knows? Who cares? Ten minutes for half a year's salary."

"Unfortunately I care."

"Come on. You ain't some hidebound type who objects to recreational drugs."

"You don't know me, Joe. I do object. And, guess what, I've still got those same three kids. Thanks for the compliment, but no way will I drive your cocaine or heroin or whatever it is across the border. You need to find somebody else."

I don't think he did get the car across. But, of course, if I'd driven it, I'd have something else to write about.

Jack called. He wasn't going to sign the papers I'd
sent to keep the divorce simple enough for me to afford a
cut-rate, $250 lawyer. "I don't want a divorce. I want to be
married to you."

I said (not analyzing whether I hoped it might be true),
"The only way you can be married to me is to get a divorce
and start over."

He reluctantly signed the papers, flew to El Paso for the
divorce, and waited in the hallway while my lawyer and I
wove through the crowd to the courtroom.

"The judge is an alcoholic, so don't give that reason
for wanting a divorce. When I feed you the question, just
answer, 'Irreconcilable differences, Your Honor.'"

It took three rote queries, three coached answers, and
less than six minutes for the judge to crack his gavel on the
walnut oval. "Divorce granted."

I drove Jack to the Puerto del Sol in Juarez for their
ceviche, and at one of the silver boutiques in the Pronof
shopping mall, he picked out an *Hecho-en-México* sterling-
fish-and-red-bead necklace for me as a starting-over gift.

Back at my house, he greeted the children but went
immediately to the Mimbres bowls on a shelf. "Why don't I
take these with me this trip? They're so fragile, they might
break when you pack everything up to come home."

"No." I decided not to address the fact that I probably
wouldn't be coming back after all. "I think they'll be all
right."

For three years in a row, Martha Foley's *Best American Short Stories* had selected a story of mine to be included in the list of "Distinctive Stories," and I accepted that the stories—all with male protagonists and sent off before my epiphany—were probably competent enough. But now I knew how to write and what to write, and I could no longer countenance a fake point of view that invalidated a story.

And I wanted to tell other writers how to write authentic stories.

But UTEP, like Rice, offered one creative writing course, taught by Francis Fugate, who subscribed to all the usual tenets of fiction writing, including the one that gave writers poetic license to write from any point of view ("Pretend to be a serial killer." "Write as if you're a Vietnamese peasant."). He taught that the art of fiction was the art of lying, and that imagination could replace experience. He didn't understand, as Eudora Welty had—and as I did by then—that writing is bad when "it isn't honest."

I also knew, as Chekhov had understood, that "a lie in fiction is a hundred times more boring than it is in life," but I wasn't teaching the class.

Nonetheless, a number of Fugate's students, who knew I also wrote, came to my office to bemoan his assignments.

One student, a former truck driver now in his sophomore year, was typical. He complained that he had no idea what the teenaged girl, whose point of view he was supposed to use, would feel. "I know what it's like to drive a cattle truck down from Cloudcroft, have the cattle shift on a curve, and know you're going over a cliff. I could tell that story. But to tell any story from inside the head of a teen-aged female—!"

That fall, Bob brought Genelle and Bryan to El Paso, and I gave a party so Bob could meet John Rechy. I'd read Rechy's novel in Colombia, and when I realized he lived in El Paso, I'd looked him up in the El Paso phone book. I'd just read a Terry Southern article that compared Rechy's *City of Night* to Bob's *One Hundred Dollar Misunderstanding*, so I knew I could keep the conversation going.

When Rechy came in, however, Honey's husband, Tom, glanced at his pumped muscles in his black T-shirt and black jeans and shouted, "Hey! Jack LaLanne!"

Rechy left at once.

He called on the phone a few minutes later. "Who's the guy in the red socks?"

"My brother-in-law."

"Well, call me when he leaves and I'll come back."

After everyone left, I called, Rechy returned, and he and Bob sat on my red chairs while I took Ken's Shakespeare chair. We drank wine and talked.

"I know I write better than Norman Mailer," Bob said, "but he's good at parties." He shook his head. "I once had some guy going around New York saying he was me, and if I could have found him, I'd have paid him to go to parties for me."

Rechy nodded. "At parties you can run into somebody like Pat's brother-in-law."

About 4:00 a.m., they had agreed to halve the Great American Novel. Rechy would take the homosexual title, Bob the heterosexual one.

Since I still wanted universality and didn't strive to write the Great American Female Novel, I didn't insist we break that division into thirds.

"You know I'm not married to Genelle, Pat." Bob
and I sat at the red enameled table over coffee. No one else
was up yet.

"In Texas, if you introduce a woman as your wife, you're
married to her."

"No shit?"

"No shit."

"You know that for sure?"

"One of the guys who was here last night is a lawyer."
He frowned. "He someone important?"

"Not very. But he called this morning and mentioned
that when Genelle introduced herself as your wife and you
let it stand, you inherited a Texas wife."

He brushed curling hair off his forehead as I'd seen him
do dozens of times. "OK, so I'm married in the state of
Texas."

"Well, she's also the mother of your son." But before
he could counter that with a compliment I couldn't quite
believe, I changed the subject. "Want to go across to Juarez
this morning?"

"I don't dare cross the border. I'm too famous. I'm on
at least one of their lists. They'd stop me and spend hours
searching for drugs."

I didn't ask who "they" were. Nor did I want to hurt his
feelings by saying that the border patrol in El Paso probably had bigger game in mind, that they'd rather stop a
Cadillac packed with cocaine than find a couple of pounds
of hash in a diaper bag.

One evening after Bob left, John Rechy gave me a copy of a new one-act he'd written. I don't remember the subject matter, but the play may have had autobiographical echoes. ("In first grade when the teacher was teaching us to count, she'd say 'One' and I'd jump up. I'd do it every time. Finally she said, 'Oh, I see. You think we're saying your name, don't you? Well, we won't call you Juan any more. From now on, you're Johnny.' Right there I lost my heritage.")

I knew about sensitive writers, how they need feedback and positive reinforcement, and I don't remember why I didn't contact Rechy. But a week or so after he'd given me the play, when I called to invite him to dinner, he said, "You ignored my work. I don't think we can be friends again."

"I'm terribly sorry." And I asked across his cold silence, "Is there anything I can do to make up that oversight?"

"I doubt it. But maybe with seven orange candles and a sacrificial lamb—," he said sarcastically as he hung up.

Fortunately it was close to Halloween, and the next day, I stopped off at a drug store near campus, found a package of orange jack-o'-lantern candles and a set of plastic farm animals. I tied seven candles and the plastic sheep together with an orange ribbon and took the bundle over to Rechy's house.

"Here." I handed it to him when he opened the front door. "My atonement."

He stared at me dumbfounded a moment before he laughed.

"OK, OK. What time is dinner?"

My second Christmas in El Paso I gave a dinner for twenty other single people, and Honey and Tom, with their two children. Honey invited her office mate in Graham Hall, Duane Carr—by then considered the best graduate student in the department—and I suspected something might be developing between them.

But I did notice that throughout the dinner, his green eyes studied me.

He said later he'd been impressed that I could cook, that I gave everyone a string of love beads (a twenty-inch strand of dyed macaroni, twenty-five cents each in Juarez), and that my children, in their red Christmas outfits, lined up to be introduced without a protest.

My colleagues continued to pair me with single men, and during the holiday, Rick, a new Ph.D. in French, was more or less my escort as ten of us went to dinner and *Satyricon*. Maureen, across the restaurant table beside Duane Carr, was obviously more interested in Rick, and when we convened at the movie theater, the grad student ended up next to me.

The film was one of the worst I ever sat through. As it ended I wished I'd spent more time in the lobby with Duane Carr, who left for innumerable drinks of water, and I said, "It takes real talent to make incest, rape, death, and destruction that boring."

The night was icy, and as we walked to the parking lot, I shared my green wool ruana with him while Maureen and Rick dodged the El Paso wind together. I thought briefly it was a shame she hadn't recognized that Rick was gay and that Duane Carr, in his wrong clothes, wasn't. But he was probably half her age anyway, and since she hadn't noticed his broad straight shoulders, slender hips, or green eyes, I didn't say anything.

I had scores of dinner invitations, and my children saw scores of male colleagues dropping by for a glass of wine or coming to take me to some faculty party.

"You interested in anyone in particular?" Shelley asked occasionally, but since I wasn't, I always shook my head.

"How about Ronnie? He's cute. He could come back," Stephanie said.

"He's barely twenty. He's much too young for me."

"Tom Green? He's cute, too."

I shook my head. "Way too young."

"How old does someone have to be?" That from six-year-old Sean, who preferred measurable quantities and preciseness.

"At least in his thirties."

So the next time the children were included in a dinner party, they surveyed the men in the room, and after dessert, Sean stopped directly in front of Duane Carr. "How old are you?"

"Thirty-six."

A few nights before, after a departmental meeting, some of us had stopped by a lounge, and he'd been carded as being too young to drink. He'd tried to convince the bartender he was actually thirty-four, but since he didn't have a driver's license, he didn't get served. His handsome unlined face, cragged by acne scars, didn't look either thirty-four or thirty-six, and I had to smile at the numbers he'd obviously plucked from thin air.

The night of Dr. Mortensen's party, Jim and Mary gave Duane Carr and me a ride, and I suppose we looked like a double date as we went in together. And of course he was attentive, refilled my wine glass, brought hors d'oeuvres, stood near me, and once leaned down unexpectedly to kiss me as I sat on the arm of Jim's chair.

Around two in the morning, we four wove to the car, and when Jim stopped at my house, I overhead him mutter to Mary as Duane Carr got out with me, "Well, with as much as he drank, nothing will happen."

He was wrong.

But while we were making love and I heard in the darkness, "What's your name?" I became abruptly sober.

The next morning when the phone rang, I knew it was my father making his Sunday call, and I didn't look at the young man next to me in bed. But as I hung up and glanced at the golden hair curling in the hollow in the center of his chest, he smiled and reached out to pull me into an embrace.

Grooves, which would have been dimples in a face less craggy, indented his cheeks on each side of his lips, and I liked his smile. His eyes up close were as deep as ever, but since he hadn't known in the night where he was or whom he was with—

I got up, showered, and came back to the bedroom to say to him, dressed in his checkered trousers and striped shirt, "I have to go, so I made you a cup of tea."

"I thought I could take you to breakfast."

"It's Paul's birthday. I have to go eat cake. Just lock the door on your way out."

The next Monday, as I waited in the coffee line of the faculty lounge, he came up beside me. "It took me all of yesterday to deal with that hangover. I don't think I ever had one that bad. Did you manage to eat chocolate birthday cake?"

"It was white. With frosting pansies decorating the top—an inside joke of Rick's—and, no, I turned green just looking at it."

He picked up a cup of coffee and a donut with brilliant red cherry filling.

I glanced at vermilion glaze. "I have to admit that makes me turn green, too."

He grinned. "Where are you sitting?"

I nodded toward a table where Paul and Nona waited with their coffee. I didn't extend an invitation, but he followed me anyway, and as we sat down, I introduced him.

Paul wore a Ralph Lauren shirt, the sweater we'd chipped in to buy for his birthday, a wide leather belt, and a leather wristband, and I knew he'd dismiss anyone in a striped green shirt, checkered brown pants, and corduroy jacket shiny at the seams. Stylish Nona, who shopped with me ("You take the lavender tunic. I'll get the blue.") was polite, but she, too, greeted the English Department's brightest graduate student with cool disdain.

I thought it significant, however, that he didn't react like a male of my generation, classifying women as virgins or whores and refusing public acknowledgment of any female he'd bedded. I thought it significant that kids his age had at least gotten beyond such nonsense and that two mornings later, he could sit and drink coffee and smile at some female with whom he'd had sex.

On Tuesday before class, Duane turned up in the faculty lounge and again joined me at a table. As he juggled his cup of coffee and saucer with another of those nauseous cherry-filled donuts, I looked away from the crimson topping and said, "It was a shame you dropped that Faulkner class. It turned out to be pretty good."

"I heard." He maneuvered his chair under the table. "It had nothing to do with you. I took a Faulkner class at Southern Colorado as an undergraduate, and I realized I didn't want to reread all those Faulkner novels."

"I guess you heard the class came up with a paper on Faulkner's comic vision."

He nodded. "About how he used Popeye and Little Orphan Annie and the funny papers to make a black comedy out of *Sanctuary*. But if that's all he's doing, making fun of his characters and his audience, then he isn't worth reading."

Even though I agreed, I said, "That sounds pretty conceited."

"You mean 'opinionated.'"

I took a swallow of coffee. "*Modern Fiction Studies* accepted the paper, and since I insisted that the names of everyone in the class had to be on it, they'll all have a publication credit. Something nice to have on a vita sheet. It's a shame you missed out."

He looked at me. "I can publish my own criticism."

I might have tired of such absolute certainty if he'd stayed in the class, but since he hadn't, I found his assurance—rare in any student, graduate or not—as intriguing as his green eyes.

I'd collected a band of friends who called at all hours.
"I'll just talk for a minute," they'd say, ignoring the fact that
another friend would telephone or drop by as soon as they
hung up. They knew about John, and they tracked my com-
ings and goings more closely than I wanted, but because El
Paso was so far from real civilization and everyone seemed
so lonely, I hated to tell them to back off.

They insisted we do things together, and they planned
dinner parties, camping trips, and excursions that included
a dozen or so members of the group. Honey usually
babysat, but if she and Tom went along for the weekend,
we hired a babysitter for our five. They began to call me
"Auntie God," a nickname Bob Gover thought up ("Since
you know everything."), and no one cared if I invited a male
colleague to go on an outing as long as he wasn't anyone I
might get serious about.

Just before a weekend ski trip to Ruidoso, to which
Mary had invited Duane Carr since he'd skied in Colorado, they decided we should all rent a house and move in
together. "No graduate students except Nona. We want a
stable group. You'll be the den mother, and we'll all help
raise your children."

I attempted to explain that I wasn't really a contented
divorcée and that in case they'd never noticed, I didn't say I
was divorced but that I was" between marriages."

They ignored that.

I nonetheless stalled renting the house, and when Rick
asked me to marry him ("We'll get a divorce, but if I have an
ex-wife and ex-children, my family will finally stop asking
when I'm getting married."), I managed to stall that, too.

A few days after the ski trip, while I read *Demian* for a next day's class, I got a call about midnight. "I'd like to talk. I wondered if you were still up."

"I'm still up."

In ten minutes he knocked on the front door in his corduroy jacket, and I handed him a bottle of wine to open (three for ten dollars from Penrod's on Mesa). I used the wine glasses I'd brought from New Orleans, and we drank and talked about literature and language. As I listened, I was charmed.

"All adjectives show human relationships. If you're kind, you have to be kind to someone. If you're cruel, it's because you're cruel to someone. Even adjectives like 'fat' and 'thin' or 'young' and 'old' are relative to someone else's size and age."

"Where did you hear that? In some other Southern Colorado University class?"

"I just thought it up as I was saying it." Duane tilted his head. "But I think it's valid."

When we finished that bottle, I found another, and I didn't mention I had to finish a Hesse novel, so it must have been around three o'clock before he got up to leave.

I walked him to the door, and he looked down at me. "I'm always surprised when I stand next to you. From a distance you look tall."

"I always thought I was five seven. My illusion of grandeur. I'm five four."

He stood silent for a minute. "You shouldn't get interested in me, you know. I'm not sure I'm capable of getting involved."

I didn't say I was acquainted with plenty of men capable of getting involved or that he was too young anyway. I merely said, "Don't worry about it."

The next evening, and the next, he called with excuses for dropping by, but since my omnipresent friends could arrive at any moment, after a week, it seemed easier for me to drive the six blocks to his apartment than for him to walk up to my place and wait for Rick or Paul or Nona to go home and for the children to fall asleep.

His was the typical cheap furnished apartment of a university town, and the clashing colors of orange chairs, turquoise sofa, and brass lamps with patterned red and white shades were even worse than his clothes. But after we made love on the turquoise plastic and wrapped ourselves in a quilt to talk, I became rather fond of the couch.

I realized I was becoming rather too fond of him as well, and over the next few days, I found myself turning down Lou and Howard.

In the previous year in El Paso I hadn't shut out any possibilities, and I knew perfectly well that sleeping exclusively with a kid in his twenties, who admittedly wasn't that involved, was foolhardy when I was nearing forty.

So I stopped at Duane's apartment and said, "I have to grade papers tonight. But before I start on them I came by to ask if you'd care if I went out with other men."

I'd made it a practice since college not to mention any-one I dated to anyone else I went out with, and this was the first time I'd mentioned even the shadow of another man.

He gazed at me a long moment. "I suppose if you feel you need to go out with other guys, then you should."

"That's not what I asked. I asked 'Would *you* care?'"

He didn't look away from my face. "Of course I'd care."

My friends sat around a table at the Kern Place Tavern and jokingly made a list of the men I had dated. Although they smirked and surmised that this new guy must be good in bed, they agreed that I might as well enjoy myself as long as it wasn't serious. And how could it be with someone that young and inexperienced? He'd never been married, and he didn't even have a master's. "Ultimately you need someone with a Ph.D.," they said, echoing friends from New Orleans who'd warned me against divorce in the first place. "You're priced out of the market with your degree. You'll never find anyone to marry who's your equal. Maybe you ought to reconsider going back to Jack."

At the tavern, they'd been documenting the pluses and minuses of every dinner date, and they didn't expect me to find a man and break up the group. Anyway, they assured me I should have someone my age or older. A rich man with the required Ph.D., L.L.D., or M.D. Someone eligible needed a tenured professorship, a medical practice, or a law firm partnership, and he had to have a pricey car, perhaps a house. "That Dr. Del Campo drives a Lincoln. He told you the first time he met you that his late wife had been Black Irish, too." And then they added, without meaning it, "He might be a good bet."

The minuses could be unruly children, hefty alimony payments, a bit of alcoholism, or a stalking ex-wife, but their list included enough men unburdened with those.

Such things as kindness, heroism, or creativity weren't on their list, so I didn't try to explain that I had a profession and that I could bring home a gorilla if I felt like it.

Nona and Ann adopted the "burnt-roll" rule for men they went with, and although Howard scoffed, "That's ridiculous. You don't quit dating somebody for that. You obviously didn't like the guy in the first place," every woman around the Kern Place Tavern table agreed that it was a perfectly valid litmus test.

We occasionally discussed the rationale for accepting a second date, and the consensus was that if you went to Juarez and your date noticed you had to reach too far across the table to dip tortilla chips in the salsa, and if—without fanfare—he moved the salsa dish closer to you, that was a definite positive.

One evening my friends gathered at my house for a chicken lasagna Honey would fix, and I stood at the kitchen sink sawing up the chicken. No one had been thrilled that Honey had again invited her office mate, but they accepted that Duane Carr had appeared in his corduroy jacket and was leaning against the counter while we discussed his class in Milton and he watched me hack through the breastbone.

"Trust me. *Paradise Lost* will get better," I said. "About Book Four when Adam and Eve come in. I took eighteen hours of Milton, and—"

The chicken slid from my fingers and dropped into the sink.

I picked it up, rinsed it, and grasped the knife again. "I don't think I'll ever read *Paradise Lost* again without a lottery prize attached, but Milton's sonnets are the best."

He reached out a slender hand and held the chicken carcass steady for me.

Perhaps it wasn't a billboard or burnt-roll moment, but it was certainly a plus.

Paul was going with an electrician, who planned to check the wiring in the house we were to rent together, and they came by with Rick to warn me that I should start dating someone more suitable than a young grad student. ("You're getting too bound up in him. He isn't worth your time."). Later, Ann stopped me in the hall. "This one's good-looking, but he's just too young. He's lying when he says he's older than twenty-three. He can't even keep his made-up age straight."

"He says he told that bartender he was thirty-four because he thought the man had asked what year he was born."

"Yeah, sure."

I smiled. "But, hey, if he wants to go to that much trouble to pretend to be thirty-six to my thirty-nine, let him. I don't mind."

They kept it up, however, and one night over a glass of Lancers rosé I said to him, "You told me you might not be able to get involved, but since we're both single, I think if I got pregnant, I'd expect you to ask me to marry you. Not that you'd have to go through with it, but just out of polite-ness, for the form of it, I'd expect you to ask."

"You'd have my baby!"

"There's too much Fate in a pregnancy," I said, "And I never tempt Fate. So of course I'd have the baby."

His eyes flashed darker green. "Then let's get married tomorrow."

When I explained that no one could marry overnight in Texas, he said, "Well then, why don't we go across to Juarez tomorrow and get an engagement ring? I have twenty dollars."

I couldn't imagine what someone could buy, even with the sagging peso, for a twenty-dollar bill, and I thought, Oh, brother. But nonetheless, I joined him after morning classes and we strolled across the Stanton Street Bridge to Juarez Avenue.

We stopped at one of the many shops featuring gold jewelry. "We're looking for an engagement ring."

The man behind the counter, who spoke impeccable English, beamed and started pulling out trays of diamond rings.

I didn't glance at them or their price tags. "Diamonds were my mother's favorite, but I've never been keen on them."

Duane smiled. "You know, neither have I."

The man went to another counter. As he put the tray on the glass top, Duane said, "There. That one."

Fashioned of tiny, rough, gold bars, it had a small pearl, not centered but set artistically on one side. The man nodded and plucked it out. "Yes. That's the one." He slipped it on my finger, where it exactly fit, before he said, "The price is $18.95."

"Hey, that'll give us enough left for four twenty-five-cent margaritas at the Kentucky Club."

Of course, I thought.

That one *was* a billboard.

I went to class wearing the Juarez gold and pearl ring. And naturally everyone up and down the hall noticed.

Mary, still waiting for Jim to propose, muttered, "I don't know why you want to get married again anyway. You have everything now."

Nona shook her head. "I don't believe it." But then she sighed and looked at Ann. "Well, I guess we better plan an engagement party."

I couldn't have thought of anything worse.

My mother, with all those creations to exhibit, had insisted I go to parties: "If you don't go to this one, they won't invite you to the next one."

One of the worst events in my life had been a seventh-grade birthday party in Tulsa to which the whole class had been invited—and to which my mother naturally pressured me into attending. But every other student in class had stayed away, and I'd had to spend the entire afternoon beside a huge cake surrounded by twenty-three nut cups, twenty-three paper plates, and crepe paper streamers, as the only guest.

And by age thirty-nine, I'd realized I hadn't wanted to go to the first party, let alone the next one.

So when Rick said to Duane—in yet another attempt to discourage him and the whole marriage idea—"You know Pat flits from party to party on three hours' sleep. What are you going to do about that?" and Duane smiled and said, "Give me a week," I certainly wasn't dismayed.

It wasn't until we went to City Hall for the license   that I glimpsed his birth certificate. Born on November 16, 1934, he was a thirty-six-year-old Scorpio.

"You're only three years younger than I am," I said. "I thought all this time I was cradle robbing."

"I knew how old I was."

I looked at the curling hair falling over his unlined forehead. "What are you doing as a graduate student? Everyone's convinced you're twenty-three."

"I didn't start college until I was almost thirty. But I guess when you aren't attached you stay looking young."

"What did you do until you were almost thirty?"

"I worked on the railroad in Colorado. As a telegrapher."

"No one's been a telegrapher since 1880."

Perhaps being in a time warp keeps you looking young as well.

And it was hard to convince any of my friends that he was old enough for me.

Except for John, whom I had to tell before he heard it from someone else.

He scowled and said at once, "He's never been married. Don't you think some guy who's gotten that old without being married must have sexual problems?"

I patted his hand. "Don't worry about it, John."

He turned his hand over quickly and grasped mine, and when he added, "If you ever write about me, be kind," I nodded.

When the political scientists at the Kern Place Tavern heard of my engagement to a graduate student, they said, "But *he* wasn't on the list!" and everyone in the group—and some who weren't—tried to talk me out of such foolishness.

I brushed aside urgings that I had to marry money or someone with a Ph.D. and my academic rank, but one argument did give me pause.

"You two walk around, gazing at each other and holding hands. But if you get married and live happily ever after, you'll never write again." Colleagues who didn't know I already had children warned me that Jane Austen and Virginia Woolf hadn't been happily married and certainly didn't have children. "It's like Tolstoy says, happy people don't have a thing to write about."

Tolstoy had actually said "happy families are all alike," but I never corrected anyone else's quotes. And besides, what if the sentiments were accurate? Writing about love and being in love were vastly different. What if being able to relax with someone I adored forced me to relinquish my illusions of being a writer?

Besides, I'd been divorced only nine months. "Why am I jumping into this?"

He tousled my hair. "We can go sit in the park and tell everyone we got married. We don't have to have a ceremony."

But as he said it, I realized I wanted to take a shot at legal marriage again.

I shook my head. "No. I guess I'll give Fate another chance. I'll go through with it."

After I told Mike and my father I was getting married, I felt obligated to notify a few males who might show up in El Paso and expect to find me single. (I often told the professors at the Kern Place Tavern—only half joking— that men lived in a state of suspended animation.)

When I called Jack and Bob, the same long silence hugged the long-distance line before each murmured, "Are you sure you want to do that?"

Ronnie, only twenty, was more adult and at least he wished me luck.

But my friends in El Paso tried again and again to sabotage the whole project.

When "He's too young" and "You need someone to provide for you" no longer worked, Nona told me at least to look around El Paso's black population for a lawyer or doctor. "You already tried a white guy."

They warned me that my Ph.D. and publications would doom a relationship with any red-blooded academic who lacked my credentials. "You, of all people, know how competitive men are. You want them to be heroic, but how can they be heroes if they're not top dog?"

"Being strong enough to be kind is the heroism I'm talking about. And besides, I don't think this man is competitive."

When all else failed, they tried cautioning him that he'd become an instant father. "She has all those children. There isn't just one. There are three of them."

He merely smiled. "I wouldn't care if there were forty."

He fortunately put a stop to the lavish backyard wedding my friends were planning ("I don't like spectacles."), but he conceded that Honey, Tom, and all the children could come to a marriage performed by a justice of the peace.

Which meant going to the police substation on Alameda Street.

So we bought wedding rings at a pawnshop near Stanton Street, and on our way to Alameda, I picked up a bouquet of salmon-colored gladiolas—which matched the polka dots in my midnight blue miniskirt—from a Mexican street vendor.

The wedding march consisted of police calls, and we stood up in the greasy aisle, flanked by two policemen and their prisoners, who had to wait until the end of the ceremony before they could be arraigned.

The Spanish-speaking JP presided with a set of vows he'd written himself that said I'd get all the groom's possessions—a Gibson guitar and thirty-five cents—while he got my undying devotion.

"Now you can kiss the bride."

Honey passed out Rice-a-Roni—even to the two traffic violators and two policemen—because she hadn't found a package of rice in her cupboard.

But no one seemed to mind the crunch of pasta and rice grains against the grimy floor as we walked to the recessional of the police radio out into the vast night.

Where the stars hung above us like the lights of planes just taking off.

Tolstoy was wrong.

The children and I abruptly became a family again. They'd always been serious kids, so I couldn't tell how joyful they might be deep down, but no one's grades dipped, no one behaved any other way than they'd behaved before, and since I believed that if the hostess was having a good time, the party was probably a success, I christened it a happy family.

It wasn't, however, like any happy family I knew.

Or that anyone in El Paso seemed to know.

In El Paso in 1971, where Fort Bliss machismo and conventional family values reigned, women worked, but mostly for pin money. And since no woman could get her own credit card without her husband's signature or cash a check of more than a hundred dollars without her husband's approval, no bank could fathom what to do about a husband who was a full-time graduate student/teaching assistant with a small stipend, who didn't own a car and who had let his Colorado driver's license lapse. No bank had any idea what to do with a professor wife who supported a family of five.

Fortunately, I was marrying someone who either didn't know or didn't pay attention to the conventions, and I wondered if he even realized my friends disapproved or that they kept trying to sink the relationship by calling in tandem every morning.

But whether he saw their intrusions as conscious or not, before the month was out, he called and canceled the phone.

Few professors at UTEP had publications: Jon Manchip White, a former OSS officer from Wales, wrote spy novels; C. L. Sonnichsen had a three-inch-thick history of El Paso from Texas Western Press; Walter Taylor had published a few articles on Faulkner; and Haldeen Braddy had been writing speculations about Chaucer's life since the year I was born.

So immediately after the wedding I applied for tenure and promotion. I assumed it would be automatic for me to make assistant professor given my book contract with Barron's for a study guide to *Portrait of the Artist*, my five published articles and six published short stories in good periodicals, and my popularity with the students.

John said, "I have copies of your publications. Just make a list of the stuff you're currently working on, that you've currently submitted, and I'll take it to the committee."

But it wasn't automatic, and I was turned down for both tenure and promotion.

When John told me, he added sympathetically, "I always said you were too good for this place. Why don't you go somewhere that will appreciate you."

I stopped by Sonnichsen's office to ask why the committee had voted as they had.

He hesitated a moment. "Well, you gave us possibilities, but you haven't published anything yet. You can't make assistant until you publish at least one article."

I realized none of them had read anything I'd written. "I see."

And of course I did.

Since I'd grown up without organized religion, I don't know how I got such a strong dose of the Puritan ethic that insists you work hard and let other people brag on you. But the afternoon I was turned down for promotion and tenure and realized that no one in the department except John was aware of my hardworking successes, I went to my office and looked at my psychedelic poster—which everyone thought my young office mate Tom Green had put up—and mentally vowed to my male colleagues, "OK, watch this."

I began a deliberate campaign to get my name and picture in the paper at least once a week. I informed the editor of the school paper about projects I was researching or critical papers I'd submitted—under the guise of spreading the word about academic excellence. When I had an article or story accepted or appearing in a journal, I'd notify the *El Paso Times* and the faculty magazine, *Nova*, to let the town and the university realize how busy our department was. Since I knew how overworked secondary school teachers were, I volunteered to read my stories in junior high and high schools and discuss short stories. I accepted invitations to judge El Paso High School debates and the town spelling bee (I fortunately had a list of the spelling words at the judge's table.), and I offered to do workshops for my female colleagues on how to write critical articles.

By the end of the semester, Robert Bledsoe, whose office was across the hall, stopped by my door. "OK. Enough. It's time to quit. We got it. Now you're going into overkill."

When Tony Stafford replaced John as head of the department, I was promoted to assistant professor. I also got a thousand-dollar raise.

Not long into the semester, however, while I stood discussing "Chrysanthemums" in a literature class, the black squares of dizziness multiplied across my sight and I knew I was going to faint.

An observant sophomore in the front row caught me before I hit the floor.

I more or less suspected what was wrong, but before I had to start wearing maternity tops with my elegant straight velvet skirts, black stockings, and three-inch heels, Dave Hall in the philosophy department stopped me before class. "The next time you feel yourself passing out, send a student for me. I have a couch in my office."

I felt I had to let my colleagues know, and when I stopped Tony in the hall to tell him I'd have to be out of class for a month sometime in January, he anticipated me. "You're pregnant?"

I nodded.

But he merely smiled. "Well, you're a real trooper. You can handle it."

Of course I could handle a fourth child, and in January, ten months after the wedding, I gave birth to a baby girl.

My friends gathered in the hospital room, and Ann went with Duane to Dillard's to pick out a dressing gown I could wear to entertain all the company.

Dr. Del Campo, the pediatrician I'd requested to look over the newborn, arrived and murmured, "You work fast, Dr. Esslinger."

Duane said—even as he beamed and admitted that he'd shouted at the top of his lungs with happiness as he drove from the hospital across Rim Road to our tiny house in Kern Place—"It doesn't matter who the father is, does it? All your children look like Honey."

Then the others said, "What are you going to name her?"

"Stanley? After my father?"

Duane shook his head. "No more Ss, please."

My friends grouped around the bed and nodded in agreement.

"How about 'Jennifer'?" Rick suggested. "That's a great elegant old name that's sort of ageless."

"I didn't think of it, but I like it. Especially for a heroine."

Duane nodded.

Unfortunately everyone else in 1972 considered it an elegant and ageless name fit for a heroine.

Will Simms had been so right about love being indivisible.

I'd never questioned the assertion, of course, but this new baby was as beautiful as the others had been, and I instantly loved her as much as I loved the rest. I've never been able to understand how a mother could favor one child—or one puppy for that matter—over another. Nor had I ever understood choosing a mate over a child, and whenever I met someone who'd remarried and had let a child go because the new parent couldn't adjust, I'd felt really sorry for them.

One problem I did have, however, was going back to teaching after a mere month.

I'd apportioned out my classes to colleagues, and when I returned to the classroom, I divided my month's salary between them. "You don't have to do that," Robert Bledsoe protested. But he'd taken on my job for a month, and since he made approximately my eleven thousand dollars a year (Even after Tony replaced John, the full professors still controlled the departmental funds and gave themselves the raises, so by the time they got around to evaluating the assistant professors, the money for equitable salaries had evaporated.), I got him to accept the money.

Duane by then had his master's and taught in the evenings at the community college, so daytimes when I had classes, he babysat Jennifer. That was the difficult part. He could stay with the newborn, and I had thoughts of being replaced. What if fathers could substitute for mothers after all? What if, like a chimpanzee baby who could bond with a rag doll, a child might forget an absent parent? What if there was no need for me?

It took the whole spring semester for me to relax and just love.

Since UTEP was a state school—and I'd had a father who considered it too selfish to take a scholarship when I didn't *really* need one—I made it a practice to critique any manuscript anyone from town brought me, and I often spent my office hours conferring with novice writers about their stories or having an impromptu critique session with half a dozen students.

Since I also taught courses from the freshman to the senior level, it wasn't unusual for me to walk into a room at the beginning of a new semester and see three or four students I'd already had. I warned repeaters, "You already know what I teach. No matter what the class title is, you know I'll say that literature has to be universal. At least once I'll say, 'to be understood is to be forgiven.' You know I think love is possible and that I'll emphasize how we need to care about other people. And I tell the same jokes."

But few students listened, and they kept signing up for my classes despite the fact that I always brought up my ideas on point of view, that I always insisted that good fiction had to be moral and gut-level honest.

Occasionally some girl in the back would raise a hand. "After I get out of this class, will I ever be able to enjoy a bad movie or a romance novel again?" Or a male student would ask, "Will I ever be able to read a novel written by a man from the woman's point of view without cringing?"

"I hope not."

"Clothes do make the man, don't they?" Mary looked across the room at him. "I never realized how good-looking Duane was when he wore those wrong clothes."

"Didn't you?"

I thought it useless to explain that observation was probably all, and I couldn't quite say that she needed to look people in the eye and try to discern what lay inside, to listen to them when they talked rather than asking herself what kind of an impression she was making. So I didn't say anything.

And when Paul saw Duane dressed in the fashionable clothes we'd bought for the wedding, he said, "Well, at least you caught a good-looking one."

"Did I?"

"You know how all of us wanted you to get a rich one."

"I didn't need one of those."

"But I suppose you did need a handsome one."

"I don't know if I did or not. I have no idea what he actually looks like."

"You've got to be kidding. With someone who looks like that?"

"I think he's beautiful. He's the most noticing and creative man I know, but I don't really have a clue what anyone else thinks about his looks."

Paul shook his head in disgust.

I'd been attracted to someone comfortable with himself, someone attentive and easy with his own sexuality, but I soon discovered that he was intelligent in a way I'd never seen. I'd known all those bright Rice students, all those professors and writers from good universities who had good backgrounds, which he didn't have, but he had a way of understanding things at gut level, of putting ideas together in new, almost uncanny ways.

I occasionally said, "You don't think like anyone else I know."

By then he'd told me about his extreme poverty background, about the chronic anger of his unemployed machinist father sitting down to a dinner of white beans and cornbread with six children and a wife he didn't love, about how he and his five siblings grew up feeling that the poor had no place in college, and I wondered if his more surreal conclusions resulted from the fact that he'd simply missed the conforming pressures of middle-class thinkers.

He did write his own critical papers and did get them published.

He also wrote short stories based on his childhood, sonnets that rhymed more easily and more convincingly than any American sonnet I'd ever read, and music from melodies he heard in his head.

"I don't know if you're smarter than everyone else or if you're just weird."

"I don't have a high IQ, you know."

"Of course you don't. Anyone who gets high marks on an IQ test has to think like other people. I'm surprised you have any IQ at all."

"**Tulsa University** is offering you three thousand dollars for a teaching assistantship?" I scanned the letter again. "That's what you make for part-time at the community college. I can take a two-year leave from UTEP, and you can end up with a doctorate for the same pay."

So that fall, we packed my furniture and artifacts, Stephanie, Shelley, Sean, and Jennifer, and left for Tulsa.

Jack's parents lived in Oklahoma City, and although I thought them unbelievably stingy (his father who said, "I don't see why my taxes should go to public schools. I already educated my kid," and his mother who was too sick to offer refreshments), they *were* the children's grandparents. Surprisingly, they offered to keep the kids while Duane and I drove to Tulsa an hour away. When we found a house and returned, I burst out, "It's only $125 a month! We'll have enough from Duane's $300 for food."

Jack's mother tucked loose hair into her gray bun and puffed powdery cheeks that resembled floured biscuits. "What about Jack's child support? Won't that help?"

I'd perfected sidestepping, but out-and-out lies stopped me. The El Paso judge had decreed fifty dollars a month per child, but after one Mimbres bowl and a Colima turtle pot sent as payments, there'd been nothing. And I had to admit there was no child support.

Her plump face froze, her cheeks washed whiter, and for a moment she gasped for breath. "He's not sending *anything?*"

When she died a few months later, I didn't speculate on whether her lifelong sickness or her only son's indifference contributed to her stroke.

At Texas Southern, Toni Wofford and I hadn't shared writing (although she did once bring in a poem about a crab who shouts at the sky, "I'm not a crustacean! I'm me!"), but we often traded books, one of which was Alfred Maund's *The Big Boxcar*, a modern *Canterbury Tales* set in a boxcar full of black vagrants. Each tells a story as they flee the South. One occupant of the boxcar is a woman, and when the train is stopped by a white mob, she pulls a young man to the ground beside the tracks and makes love to him to divert the mob. The mob shines a flashlight on them to watch, but the diversion works, and later, as the train carries them all safely away, the young man falls in love with the woman for her courage and sacrifice.

When I picked up a copy of *The Bluest Eye* by Toni Morrison, I recognized her immediately from the book jacket. And when I started reading how the black girl ripped apart the blond baby dolls she got for Christmas, I was completely awed by Toni's depiction of black rage. This was gut-wrenching writing at its best.

Then I got to the scene in which Cholly makes love to a girl in the woods. A white mob comes upon them, catching them in the flashlight beam, and Cholly, overcome with rage, vents his hatred not on the mob but on the girl, and subsequently all black women. Which explains the rape of his own daughter.

I finished the book and sat back in disappointment.

Toni had used someone else's scene.

And a male perspective that might or might not be true for a black male.

Somewhere along the way, I realized I could still write about men. I could create any number of male characters if I stayed out of their heads and viscera and reported what they said and did.

That's the way every woman decides what a man thinks and feels anyway—by observing what he does and says. If a writer chooses the right actions and dialogue, then readers should also be able to conclude what the character is thinking and feeling.

And now that I knew what I had to write and how I should write it, I didn't waste time on false starts.

I also saved time because Duane turned out to be a superb critic.

Before I ran into him, I'd had to stash stories in a drawer for a couple of months before I could edit them as if someone else had written them. But now I could finish a rough draft, then let him, the critic I lived with, read the story and give me an opinion.

I'd been charmed by his unusual insights, but now I learned to trust his literary instincts. If he said a story wasn't good, I revised it or tossed it. If he said a story was ready, I sent it off.

So in Tulsa, I published my first story, "The Party"—about that seventh-grade debacle and written from the female point of view—in *The Southern Review*.

It was the first story of mine that Martha Foley included in her twenty selected stories of *Best American Short Stories*.

And somehow I felt that inclusion helped justify not only what I had to write but also what I needed to say about writing.

While Duane was taking a course in *Ulysses,* I reread
the book myself.

I knew more Irish history by then, and abruptly I realized Joyce was using the Tyrone War—from its opening
battle to the Irish defeat at Kinsale and the Flight of the
Earls—to tell the story of Bloom and Molly. In fact, he was
propping his entire narrative on the references to Irish history.

Blazes Boylan, having an affair with Molly (the embodiment of Ireland), stands in for the Irish rebel Hugh O'Neill
(a Tyrone with a crest containing the Red Hand of Ulster),
who leaves a red handprint on Molly's buttocks. Bloom
merges with the historical Henry Flowers who helped
defeat the Irish, boats wait on the Liffey for the Earls, and
the famine hovers in the blackened potato Bloom carries.
When Molly ends her monologue by deciding to stay with
the impotent Bloom ("He's a man like Ireland wants."),
Joyce offers the bleak conclusion that Ireland is paralyzed
and blighted.

In college I'd defended Joyce and had insisted that if
someone on a desert island could have only one book, that
book should be *Ulysses.* I'd known *Ulysses* was limited by a
lack of empathy and a plot hard to follow without a guide,
but now I realized something else was wrong: a reader had
to bring everything *to* the novel rather than taking anything
from it. The reader had to come to the book knowing Irish
history and Irish myth if she or he wanted to understand
the narrative.

The editors of the scholarly Irish journal *Eire-Ireland* may
or may not have seen those reservations in the critical paper
Duane and I wrote together on *Ulysses,* "Hugh (Blazes) Boylan: The Last O'Neill," but they nonetheless published it.

In 1973 my father came to Tulsa to see us.

He'd always loved babies, and he carried Jennifer around, cradling her head in the crook of his arm while he rocked her to sleep for naps, for bedtime.

He drank more than ever, and before the baby was hard asleep, he'd put away at least two bourbons with their sprinkling of water. But since I let him have bourbon after bourbon anyway, we sat up every night of his visit and talked.

My mother had been dead for six years, he was only sixty-four, and he wanted to discuss dating again.

"I'm lonely. I'm going to retire in May, and I need to meet someone before I leave the company. I'm an executive there, and the Standard Oil Building is the one place in Houston I can impress a woman."

He told me that after leaving Tulsa, he'd go to Los Alamos to see Mike and to Kentucky to see his last living cousins. He saw Honey weekly since her husband had been RIF'd from the army, and she and Tom had bought a house in Pasadena, around the corner from him. "I want to see Ireland, too, so I'm going to Ulster one of these days."

"Ulster's in Northern Ireland. Why would you go there?"

"That's where our ancestors are from. The O'Moores were High Kings. Like the O'Neills."

I hadn't heard that before, but I didn't challenge it. I merely nodded.

My father had been retreating from life for six years, and he no longer seemed to enjoy anything. He'd once liked to play the patriarch and take all of us out for steak at expensive restaurants in Houston, which he paid for with a flourish of hundred-dollar bills. But after he had a small heart attack and my mother died, he gave up rare T-bones for the chicken he baked on Sunday and ate all week. He seemed smaller, lighter every time I saw him. He'd occasionally played poker when my mother went out to bridge games, but without her there to come home when he did, he gave up cards as well. About the job that had taken him to the seventeenth floor he said, "They're replacing all the men who actually know something with college graduates who've never been on a rig." And with the excuse of avoiding the heavy freeway traffic, he went to the office at three in the morning and left again right after lunch.

I don't think he even cared for the bourbons, which he poured and drank until he could no longer stand or pronounce any of his favorite Latinate words.

One summer when I visited him, I saw that the birthday and Christmas presents we'd all sent still lay on the kitchen table, unopened.

And barely a month after he left Tulsa, Honey called to say that she'd gone to his house and found him dead. "He'd broken a rib and unwrapped it. I think it punctured his lung."

I knew how unhappy he was, and I could understand if he'd untaped his rib in either an unconscious or a deliberate suicide attempt.

But I did wish he'd had a chance to see Ireland. And to have a date.

When I was reading background for the Joyce paper, I was struck by the fact that while scholars accepted that Joyce had used his wife, Nora Barnacle, as the model for the relatively docile Molly Bloom, Nora herself seemed much less compliant. When Carl Jung read *Ulysses* and complimented Joyce on how well he understood women, Nora snorted that her Jim didn't know a thing about women. I also ran across a scene in which Hemingway, helping Joyce stagger home one evening, met Nora at the door. She looked at them both and said scathingly, "Well, well, if it isn't the great writer, Ernest Hemingway, bringing home the great writer, James Joyce, dead drunk."

I liked her sarcasm and her independence.

And since few Joyce scholars seemed interested in her, I thought perhaps I could write her biography.

I read everything I could find on her, and then I applied for a summer National Endowment for the Humanities Award so I could travel to Cornell to read Joyce's unpublished love letters to her.

The letters didn't contain much about their relationship, and although they contained more intimate information than anyone could ever want to know about Joyce's own preoccupations (I could see why Nora burned most of them.) Nora remained elusive.

The outlines of her life—even before she ran off with Joyce to the Continent ("No one who has any self-respect stays in Ireland.")—were shadowy, so the next Christmas, Duane and I left the children with Honey and flew to Europe for the express purpose of tracking down Nora Barnacle Joyce.

We followed the route James and Nora Joyce traveled from Galway and Dublin to London, then to Paris and Trieste.

I'd written ahead to people who'd been acquainted with the Joyces, and in an achingly frigid December—as a fierce wind swirled ice crystals off the sea into the heart of Trieste—we stopped to see Italo Svevo's daughter. She lived in an austere mansion set back from the street, and after we rang the bell and she called down from the second floor for us to come up, we climbed the icy stone staircase.

She stood waiting at the archway to a parlor, an elderly woman in a floor-length black dress, leaning on a black cane. "I thought we would have a brandy in here."

There was no fire in the fireplace, and her biscuits had the consistency of hardtack, but I'd never seen a real Degas—a five-by-eight-inch oil-on-canvas of a reclining woman—hanging on someone's living room wall before.

It turned out that our hostess didn't remember much about Nora, however, and after an hour of small talk about her father, about his and Joyce's relationship, she pointed to the framed photos of her sons on the side table. "That was our oldest. I watched him march off to the Russian front with his unit. They were wearing summer uniforms." Her blue-veined hand floated above another silver frame. "This was our youngest. He fought with the partisans. No one was able to reach the Americans before they shelled the hotel that was partisan headquarters."

The other person I'd contacted in Trieste didn't re-member much about Nora Joyce either, but he was delight-ed to take us sightseeing at Miramar, the Hapsburg castle, whose turrets rose beside the sea. As he showed us around the icy lawns and through the equally icy rooms, he told us about the family, particularly the handsome Maximilian, briefly Emperor of Mexico, while he defended Mussolini ("The trains all ran on time when he was in power."). He insisted that few Americans understood Italians, either during World War II or in the present. But he was exceed-ingly gracious, and when at last we had to catch our train to Zurich, he took us to the station.

"Surely you are not traveling third class! No tourists go third class."

But it was New Year's Eve, and only third-class tickets were available. So we waited in the grimy lower-class wait-ing room for our not-quite-on-time train.

At Milan we changed trains and went into another greasy room dominated by a huge digital clock and a waft-ing odor of garlic. The minutes, then the hours, swept past the little glass windows of the clock until 23:59 rolled into view. When those numbers disappeared, four zeroes hung for sixty timeless seconds until finally 01 appeared in the last two slots, the new year began, and we could breathe again.

Just then a group of young Italians carrying wine bottles went by, and one of them stopped, held out his bottle with a halting English, "Ha-a-pp-y New Ye-ar."

I took the bottle, and even as I wanted to wipe off the rim, I didn't. I took a swig of the red wine and smiled at the Italian teenager, whom I felt I understood.

When we reached Zurich we were relieved to find that the hotel—unlike the one in Trieste—wasn't under reconstruction, that the rooms had fresh towels and soap, and that hot water actually poured from the taps in the bathroom.

Joyce had died in Zurich in 1941, Nora in 1951, and we wandered among the cemetery gravestones and statuary until our feet began to freeze. Then we went to the restaurant where the Joyces had eaten their meals, and I talked to the owner (*"Ja.* That was their table by the window. Frau Joyce sat in the same place after her husband died. She liked my Wiener schnitzel."), and to two older women who'd been young waitresses in World War II. ("Ah, *ja,* Frau Joyce. She was a nice lady.")

Our last stop was the British Museum where I read a last stack of Joyce papers.

Unfortunately, as I read Nora's few handwritten notes and her final yellowed letters that contained a loyal defense of her late husband ("Sure, if you've been married to the greatest writer in the world, you don't remember all the little fellows."), what emerged was someone I no longer liked. She might have been sarcastic, but even though she once said to Joyce, "If God Almighty came down to earth, you'd have a job for him," she nonetheless accepted Joyce's utter dependence on other people's money. And after Joyce died, she became the same kind of parasite herself, pleading with Sylvia Beach, cajoling Harriet Weaver to send money.

I realized I didn't want to study her for the years required to write a biography, and although my agent kept salivating for the manuscript ("I can sell that one, Pat!"), by the end of the trip, I'd scrapped my plans for a biography of Nora Joyce.

Instead of writing a biography of Nora Barnacle Joyce, I contacted Frederick Ungar to see if I could do a book for their playwrights' series on Sean O'Casey, who hadn't disappointed me. The editor wrote back that she had O'Casey covered, but that the author who'd been researching George Bernard Shaw had copped out. "Would you consider doing that one?"

I said I would, but I worried that since cleverness is often accompanied by a cruel streak, I might be disillusioned by Shaw, too.

Nonetheless I began reading his plays, letters, essays— even his music criticism—and the secondary sources. Among them all I didn't sense selfishness, envy, cynicism, or cruelty, and I ended up appreciating his open-hearted satire, his belief in love, and his commitment to reform even more by the time I finished writing the little volume (to a specific format) than I'd liked him when I started.

I finished the manuscript in what the editor confided was record time.

As I was making the final edit, Frederick Ungar himself wrote to say that he disliked hyphenated names. ("Pick 'Esslinger' or 'Carr.' I don't like 'Esslinger-Carr.'") I'd never been overly fond of "Esslinger" myself, so I chose "Pat M. Carr."

I'd already made the mistake of using different publishing names: "Pat Moore," "Pat Esslinger" (where *Contemporary Authors* sends readers to find me before 1971), "Pat Esslinger-Carr," "Pat M. Carr," and finally—after I recalled how Nathanael West in *Miss Lonelyhearts* had mocked women with three names, "Pat Carr."

There turned out to be some half a dozen Pat Carrs who are writers or singers and who publish, but at least—and at last—I'd settled on a name.

I'd always thought the sand-colored adobes and surrounding desert made El Paso one of the most romantic cities in America, and I was delighted to return to it.

Of course I also returned to the English Department, which in the two years I'd been away had begun a creative writing major, headed by Les Standiford, a creative writing Ph.D. from Utah.

The men were as possessive of course offerings as ever, however. And even though this time I was awarded tenure and a permanent place on the graduate faculty, despite my stories in good journals, including *The Southern Review*, *Arizona Quarterly*, and *Best American Short Stories*, Les denied my request to teach a fiction writing class.

But 1975 had become a time of awareness and rising female consciousness, and the women on campus began to notice that the men in every department took home twice as much pay as they did. They brought a class action suit against the university, and when the lawyers suggested that each woman be paired with a comparable male colleague to assess accomplishments and salary—and no male English assistant professor had a single publication—the department patriarchs were forced, reluctantly, to promote me to associate.

They also permitted me to teach a couple of graduate classes—which, of course, didn't add a dollar to my salary, but which did let me influence students who were going out to teach.

Recalling my mistake, I encouraged female writers to stick to their maiden names or to make up a name, no matter how extravagant. And most women writers—never a male—asked how I juggled marriage, teaching, and writing.

"I'm afraid you do have to be married to the right man."

The females—no males ever—would also occasionally say, "Someone told me you have four kids. Is that true? How can you write with four children in the house?"

"When I'm writing and they interrupt, I ask them to let me finish a scene. I tell them that unless the house is on fire, I want them to go watch the clock and come back in fifteen minutes. Then they'll have my undivided attention. They all learned how to tell time pretty fast."

I read as rapidly as ever, and though still unable to spell, I graded essays as quickly, so I wrote in the mornings before class and on Sundays. And after Duane finished his dissertation, we sat at the round oak dining table and composed novels—his, *The Bough of Summer*, about his days on the railroad, and mine, *The Grass Creek Chronicle*, using Heart Mountain and World War II.

It's a truism of publishing that no publisher ever comes knocking, asking for your manuscript. So I was astonished one evening to go to the door and have the young man on the porch say, "I heard you and your husband were writers. I'm starting a press here in El Paso, and I'd like to look at something of yours."

I swallowed.

Then I managed to say, "As a matter of fact we each have a novel."

So in 1976 I had two books appear. *Bernard Shaw*, published by Frederick Ungar in New York, and *The Grass Creek Chronicle*, brought out in a matched set with *The Bough of Summer* by Endeavors in Humanity Press in El Paso.

I hadn't thought much about reviews. Various readers had called my story "The Party" "exquisite" or "breathtaking feminism," but now I had books to be reviewed.

"Ask someone from the university, Pat," the editor of Endeavors said. "I'll send them galleys, and we can bring out the reviews with the books."

Les Standiford volunteered to read my book, and I asked Jon Manchip White if he'd review Duane's. "But if you're at all hesitant, don't do it." He tapped his British walking stick, beamed, and a few days later sent a note, written in elegant rose-colored ink, that his review had been sent to the paper.

Both reviews appeared on Easter Sunday, and I brought in *The El Paso Times* so we could savor them over coffee and hot cross buns. Les waxed effusive, calling my book "intense, uncompromising, and true," but Jon wrote that while the basically autobiographical main character of Duane's novel had sexual prowess, he was ultimately "an amiable but dull young man."

Duane was understandably dashed. But all he said was, "He's obviously in love."

"Nonsense."

But then I remembered how Jon had startled me the day of the creative writing faculty photo shoot by putting his hands around my waist and lifting me onto a wall to stand beside him.

I'd never minded someone being fond of me, but to have it blazoned in *The El Paso Times* was a disclosure I hadn't seen coming. I could have handled a bad review of my own book, but this putdown had hurt the one person I'd been looking for all my life.

I considered mailing Jon a white feather, but while I did consider his action cowardly, a feather somehow didn't seem quite appropriate, so instead, I sent him to Coventry. I knew that he, as an Englishman, would understand the working-class insult of "sending a mate to Coventry," that punishment of silence, in which every worker in the plant ignores the person who has violated the lower-class ethics of the workplace.

And of course Jon understood perfectly.

At the next faculty party, he stopped Duane in the kitchen and said he hoped the review had been all right because he'd really liked the book. Duane assured him that it was fine, and Jon came from the kitchen, smiling, having made everything up, preparing for me to acknowledge him again.

"When you left the party without looking at him, you should have seen his face," Duane said as we walked home. "He was devastated. How could you do that to him?"

"That question has just a hint of male bonding."

He protested, but I nonetheless didn't try to explain that I'd considered Jon both a colleague and a professional writer. I'd trusted him, and I'd made a point of giving him a way out if he hadn't wanted to pen a decent review.

As far as I was concerned, it had been a serious betrayal.

The corner windows in my office in Hudspeth Hall
overlooked the sluggish trickle of the Rio Grande and the
tiny adobe houses scattered like pink and blue dice on the
dry Juarez side of the river, and I often stared across what
had once been a mighty river toward the sad cubes of
Mexican huts.

That day, before my one o'clock class, as I stood con-
templating the barren hill with my typical American guilt, I
got a phone call. "This is John Leggett from the University
of Iowa. I want to let you know you won the 1977 Short
Fiction Award."

I'd heard about the Iowa Short Fiction Award—a
thousand dollars and publication—just before the entry
deadline, and I'd called my agent to suggest we submit the
manuscript of my new story collection, *The Women in the
Mirror*. She said there wasn't enough money in it for her to
get involved, but she added that I could send the collection
if I wanted, so I packaged up a Xerox of the copy I'd sent
her and shipped it off. A few months later, I got a postcard
advertising the new Iowa Award winner, Buz Poverman, and
beyond thinking that was certainly a tacky way to notify
entrants they'd lost, I filed in my trash can the card and all
thoughts of the contest.

But it turned out that Buz Poverman had won the award
for the previous year.

And I'd won that year's.

I'd never seen the University of Iowa. I didn't know
anyone who'd gone to Iowa except Mabel back at Texas
Southern. A series of readers and then Leonard Michaels,
the final judge, had chosen my manuscript from words on
the photocopied page.

Which was the way literature was supposed to work.

I arrived in Iowa City to see in the paper that a famous native son had died, that the funeral for MacKinlay Kantor would take place on Saturday. Ordinarily I might have looked Tim up, but my time had been tautly scheduled, so I didn't mention him—or his father—to the press people as we attended parties, interviews, and the awards ceremony.

At which the University of Iowa chef outdid himself.

Pyramids of papaya, fresh pineapple, and sweet pepper chunks, cheese cubes, and stuffed mushrooms lined the tables beneath a glittering Zeus-sized swan carved from ice. The red, yellow, green fruits and vegetables sparkled, the baked brie in spinach nests gleamed, and only late in the evening, when water dripped from the swan's beak onto beds of petit fours and crab puffs, did some of my enthusiasm for ice sculptures wane.

That same weekend John Cheever had come to give a reading, and when John Leggett brought him by for mini-quiches ("Remember, Pat, Cheever came to *your* party."), the girl reporter interviewing me for the college paper rushed to talk to him.

A few minutes later she returned, her eyes tearing up. "I'd read his biography and I admired him so much. But when I complimented him on how well he was controlling his drinking, he turned downright vicious."

Authors want to be complimented for having written your favorite story, but I couldn't say that. So I said, "Some people get defensive about being alcoholics."

She left the party soon after, but in a few minutes, she was back carrying a small wooden plaque with a collage of two children holding hands. I knew it was a keepsake she'd brought from home. "You aren't rude," she said softly as she handed it to me.

In the Iowa City radio station and newspaper interviews, I got a chance to explain my theory that point of view can make or break a story.

"But don't you have to tell the reader what a character is thinking?"

"It's a matter of showing, not telling. In *Of Mice and Men* we know what George and Lenny are thinking by what they do and say. If a character slams his fist on the table and yells, 'God damn it!' we can assume he's angry."

"And you say that men shouldn't write from inside a female's head?"

"That's what I keep saying."

"But what about Shakespeare? He wrote brilliant women characters."

"He's never inside the women's heads. He's writing drama, which is always action and dialogue. Just like film. They're both dramatic and exterior and stay out of people's heads. Shakespeare wrote those brilliant women characters from the outside."

"But don't we need to know what fictional characters are thinking and feeling?"

"To tell the reader, 'She felt sad,' rather than showing her sadness is easy writing. Choosing the right actions and dialogue is the difficult part. Hemingway said that hard writing is easy reading. And it certainly is when an author *shows* the way I want him to. Both the author and reader have to stay awake."

Finally I also got to expound on my belief that characters need to be heroic.

"You mean they have to go out and fight wars or lions?"

"No. They have to be strong enough to be kind, to care. That's what heroism is."

But that concept involved love, and it was nearly as hard to explain.

In June I got an invitation to join Ursula Le Guin, David Ignatow, Ishmael Reed, and Stanley Elkins at the Bloomington Writers' Conference, where Ishmael and I would teach a joint fiction session.

I found out the first evening that Ishmael was a friend of Bob Gover's. "Did you know, Pat, that he hasn't written in a long time?"

"I think he's probably running out of Monopoly money by now, too."

"Monopoly money?"

"His royalties. They never were very real to him. He grew up in an orphanage, and I guess that makes you regard money differently than the rest of us."

I think Ishmael regarded money the way most of us did, and he reminded me of a successful man used to a comfortable income—and even more used to being taken care of by women. In fact, in our first seminar session, he noticed that he had a leaking Styrofoam cup. "Look at that! My coffee's running all over the table."

I could tell it was a hint for me to rescue his cup and mop up the table. But my own consciousness had been raised too much by then, and even though I had to grab the edge of the table until my knuckles whitened, I managed to sit still and look at the coffee flooding the polished table and threatening the pile of manuscripts.

Finally one of the girls snatched up the cup and hurried out for paper towels.

I resisted taking care of him for the whole week, and at our last session, he said, "You know, we ought to do this together again sometime. We make a terrific team."

I smiled at him. "So we do."

Each night, two conference directors read in the auditorium, and I've always meant to copy Ursula's generous response, a simple murmur of "Thank you" as she took a hand of the reader in both of hers.

We also held discussion sessions where we exchanged theories about writing before the students, and Stanley Elkins, as one of the most venerable writers there, gave his opinions with the confidence of someone who'd been doing it for decades. "If I don't know what a palm tree looks like, I go to the encyclopedia and look one up."

Scott Saunders, the moderator, nodded toward me. "What about you, Pat?"

I'd stumbled onto what I should write. And since I recalled perfectly the banana palms in Cali with their pink blossoms that resembled the male sex organ, the palm trees in New Orleans that battered their fronds into frayed shreds under hurricane-strength rain and wind, I looked at Scott and said, "I don't trust photographs or the descriptions in an encyclopedia. Just the way I don't trust TV or films. You're getting the photographer's or some other writer's idea of a palm tree. If I want to use a palm tree in a story, I go find one."

As usual, the professors and writing students in the audience objected. But I was used to arguing about setting as well as about point of view. And as I added, "Our olfactory sense is our strongest sense, and whatever site we describe has to smell right," I couldn't help recalling the Canal Street Station, the anteroom of iron bars just outside the drunk tank, and the stench of urine.

When a novice writer asks if he or she needs to get an agent, I have to admit that I haven't a clue.

"Most New York houses won't look at a submission unless an agent sends it. Ursula Le Guin insists that New York publishers are a diminishing breed, taking only the next blockbuster, which is a replica of last year's blockbuster, and that one of these days, small presses and university presses will pick up the slack. But if you want to limit yourself to New York publishers, I suppose you have to have an agent."

I'd gotten another agent myself a few years after I naïvely gave up McIntosh & Otis, and although she tried to place my two novels and a couple of my short story collections, she had no luck either.

By then I knew better than to dump an agent as long as she was willing to keep trying, but after perhaps a dozen years—with no results—I contacted a third, then a fourth agent. At last I agreed to go with a fifth, my friend Barbara Kouts, who'd spent two or three years persuading me to let her agency see my work.

I'm not sure she expected as many manuscripts as I sent her, but she gamely took them on and started submitting to publishers.

Without any luck.

Of course I was as out of step with the literary world as I'd been with my contemporaries in high school, but I never anticipated that of all the agents I had over the years—continuously from the time I got the first—not one of them could ever sell a sentence for me.

I jumped at the chance to teach summer school and make some extra money, but the extraordinary thing that happened in the summer of 1978 was that I finally learned how to teach.

I'd never actually believed in the concept of "special" students who came to class prepared, yet I'd been relying on the fact that some students *did* read and that there were generally enough of them to carry a discussion. But while I was teaching a July class of sophomores, I realized that if I assigned an essay, gave a ten-point quiz at the beginning of every hour, and stipulated that the quizzes added up at the end of the semester for a final grade, then the whole roomful of students would have to read. They could defend their answers on the quiz ("There's no right answer if you can support it with the text," I repeated.) as we dissected the work, and the whole class could join the conversation.

It turned out I hadn't just discovered a teaching method; I'd discovered magic.

By the third day, every student had devoured every word. Some mornings, they arrived early to anticipate questions, argue over passages, and ask each other—and me when I walked in—if we'd drawn the same conclusions. Every student came out of the class with an A or a B.

When the dean called me in to question my grade inflation ("You're giving too many As."), I said I wasn't *giving* anything but that the students were earning the grades. "I'll put a set of quizzes in your box so you can see if I've missed anything."

As with *Dutchman*, he sent back the quiz papers without a word and never mentioned grades again.

In the fall, Les Standiford at last conceded to assign me a fiction writing class.

In the meantime, he'd decided we needed to extend our offerings, so he got funding for another instructor.

Among the writers he invited to campus was Bruce Dobler, whose novel about the Alaska pipeline, *The Last Rush North*, had just come out with Little, Brown. Bruce had done his homework and he knew exactly what everyone in the department wrote and published. Since he also knew enough not to blab too much about his own work, he was the best interviewee we had, and all of us urged Les to hire him.

But Bruce had written the women characters in his Alaskan novel from inside their heads, so naturally, as soon as he got to El Paso and started teaching, he and I disagreed on what students should write, on how they should write, and even on how we should grade the course.

"We shouldn't encourage people who haven't got what it takes to be writers, Pat. In fact we should discourage them by passing out Fs."

"Giving students an A or an F on their stories is like grading their souls."

"Oh, hey, in that case, I'll let my students out of class and give them all As, too."

"Come on, Bruce, I expect the stories to be the best they can write. But I assign readings, they take quizzes, and they get their final grades by adding up the numbers."

He raised unconvinced eyebrows, but I added, "Besides, anyone who wants to write will write no matter what we do. Writers don't need our As or our Fs. The person you're calling 'a real writer' doesn't need us one way or the other."

The male creative writing faculty did allow me to teach a fiction class ("The Iowa Award you won is the one Cyrus Colter won, isn't it?" "You just won the Texas Institute of Letters Short Story Prize, didn't you?"), but they were still too protective to let me have input on the graduate creative theses.

So when Jim Stowe wrote a novel, *Winter Stalk*, for his thesis, the men in the department judged it—almost in secret sessions—and not until it had been published by Simon & Schuster and Shelley gave it to me for Christmas did I get a chance to read it.

The novel's incentive moment occurs in the midst of a winter blizzard when a couple with a sick child must brave the storm to get their infant to a hospital as soon as possible. Their car skids off the highway, they hike through the snow, desperate to find help, and end up at the house of the killer. The suspense revolves around the dual questions of, Will they survive, and will they be in time to save their violently ill baby?

Jim had obviously not researched childhood illnesses, and he chose impetigo as the life-threatening disease.

Unfortunately, impetigo is a rash in babies about as serious as a pimple on a teen. If any man on the committee had had a child, someone might have corrected that. Or possibly if they'd let a woman sit in with them—

A woman might also have caught the fact that when the couple breaks through the drifts to the isolated farmhouse where the woman inside is doing a homely chore, that chore shouldn't have been shelling summer peas in the dead of winter.

No S & S editor noticed either mistake. But perhaps they, too, were all men.

Bruce stayed a couple of years, but the next fall, Les also hired Raymond Carver.

Ray was more laid back than Bruce, and the second semester when Tess Gallagher came to live with him, he blossomed into sociability. He, too, often wrote from a woman's point of view, but he didn't resist what I taught with any rancor, and even though he persisted in reading his story "Fat" with its point of view of the waitress who thinks obsessively about her obese customer, he and I never argued about it.

We merely had friendly lunches in Juarez, where we talked about writing and Chekhov.

"Anyone who reads literature, anyone who believes in the transcendent power of art . . . sooner or later has to read Chekhov."

I nodded. "And when it comes time for me to keel over, I want to go like Chekhov and have another bottle of champagne."

When Martha Foley died, the editorship of the *Best American* anthologies passed to famous authors and the writers who courted them. Once again, "who you know" rang loud and clear across the yearly anthologies. Ray asked one afternoon if I'd published anything he could recommend for a Pushcart Prize, and later when he got appointed the famous author/editor for *Best American Short Stories,* I wished I'd still been in a corner office down the hall from him.

I also wished he hadn't died before I read "Errand," his story about the death of Chekhov. I knew he didn't need me to say it, but I wished I could have told him anyway that showing what the characters did and said was exactly right, and that the young male waiter who observes the dropped champagne cork was a perfect point-of-view choice.

Given the long line of townspeople who trotted in
with manuscripts for me to look over ("Would you read this
and tell me what I'm saying?"), I wasn't particularly surprised
one afternoon as I sat in my office, reviewing notes for an
evening seminar, to see a young construction worker stride
in with a sheaf of wrinkled papers.

He stopped before the desk in a white sleeveless un-
dershirt, work pants, and steel-toed boots speckled with
exterior paint. His deeply tanned bare arms glittered with
sweat and white stucco dust, and a red bandana held back
his Indian-straight black hair as he put the pages on my
desk. "I heard you were a writer. I need some feedback on
these." He stared down at me with bold dark eyes. "I'll be
working on the new liberal arts building for a couple of
weeks. When can I come back?"

"How about this time next week."

He nodded, turned, and went out.

"Who was that?" Ray Carver came to my door.

I looked at the top page of the manuscript. "It says here
that it was Doug Gilb. He works in construction. I have the
feeling he may come by your office, too."

"Thanks for the warning."

But strangely enough, the stories weren't bad.

And even though I knew perfectly well that the young,
Native American–looking construction worker didn't need
either our encouragement or discouragement to be a writer,
both Ray and I wrote notes on the stories that told him to
keep writing.

Les decided UTEP should have a literary magazine.

"We'll exchange stories with other editors and we'll get our stuff out there, too."

And even as I thought, Oh, brother, I told him to come by our adobe house with poet Bob Burlingame with his new wife to make plans for the publication.

Bob suggested that first we make a list of the famous people we knew.

"Wouldn't it be better to have a list of famous people who know us?" I asked.

He ignored that as he replenished his drink.

A few drinks later, while we were still in the preliminary discussion stages, I realized that he and Les had obviously had some earlier altercation, and that Bob was demanding Les give him a yes or no answer to some question he'd asked.

"I can see it both ways."

"I don't want to hear both ways, I just want a damned yes or no." Bob gave a bellicose rattle to the ice in his fourth glass of rum and Coke.

"I'm not going to give you a yes or no."

I was rather proud of Les's stubbornness, but in that moment, with another blazing insight, I remembered that Burlingame was a Scorpio, his wife was a Scorpio, Les was a Scorpio, and of course, Duane, who leaned back on the cream-colored velvet couch and watched the joust, was a Scorpio. I was in the book-lined den with four of them.

No way could I work with that many Scorpios.

But fortunately, after that evening, no one mentioned a literary magazine again.

Ray Carver left after a year and Les hired Arturo Vivante, famous (in New York at least) for his stories in *The New Yorker*. I approved when he, as a former physician, tried to convince novice mystery writers that a killer can't tear a windpipe from a throat with his bare hands, but when he, like Dobler, argued that a creative man could write just as well as a woman in the female point of view, he and I disagreed. A lot.

Not as much, of course, as Gordon Lish and I did when he came for the weeklong conference Les organized that summer.

I'd had plenty of time to brainwash my street-smart students, so when Lish came, flaunting his editorship of *Esquire* and his cigarettes (I had emphysema from Jack's Salems, and the department deferred to my lungs with a smoking ban), and contending he *would* smoke in class no matter what anyone said, that he *would* have writers write from everyone's point of view no matter what anyone said, my students rebelled.

"If you have to smoke, then we'll go sit outside."

Since the whole class met the next day on the grass, there was nothing Lish could do but follow them out. And since they refused his theories on point of view, there was also nothing he could do but let them write stories the way they—and I—wanted.

On Wednesday as I crossed campus and the students on the lawn motioned me over, Lish's blue eyes looked directly at me as he said, "We all just do the best we can."

And on Thursday, when he got a letter from *Esquire* and his watery blue eyes had to read that he'd been replaced as the editor, I suspected his week in El Paso had turned into the worst nightmare of his life.

Les had a list of writers he wanted students—and himself, of course—to meet, so he invited Max Apple, Grace Paley, and Mark Medoff to campus. The students remained unimpressed except with Mark. He hadn't yet written his Tony winner, *Children of a Lesser God*, but he paced so flamboyantly in his lace-up knee boots and flowered shirt that the students liked him. And when he said, "I had to make it by the time I was thirty-five," we all merely smiled and no one asked, "Did you?"

But they did challenge Leslie Silko.

In her lecture, when she said that no Anglo should ever write from the Native American point of view, the class glanced at me with subtle, approving nods.

But then she read her story of an Eskimo woman—written from the woman's point of view. The students politely listened. When the applause died down, however, one of them raised a hand. "How come you don't want us to write from your point of view but you narrated your story as if you were an Eskimo? You aren't an Eskimo."

"Eskimos are Native Americans."

They looked back at me. "Dr. Carr?"

They waited, and I was forced to say, "Native Americans from New Mexico and those from the Yukon are different. The former know the Pueblo culture and sensibility, but they don't really know an Eskimo's deepest thoughts, hopes, or fears."

"We're all Native Americans," she repeated stoutly.

It was useless to explain that someone from the desert would never be able to distinguish twenty different kinds of Arctic snow, so I didn't try.

Les brought in Robert Bly, Jim Dickey's old nemesis, but since I didn't want to enter their ancient arguments, I didn't mention I knew Jim. And since Bly didn't write fiction, I didn't need to bring up my pet theory that invariably invited argument.

My students, however, disputed most of what he said.

As they did with David Slavitt, another "famous" New Yorker, who came to read, conduct a class, and then award the students their prizes from Les's literary contest.

Slavitt, overweight, pompous, and pretentious, alienated everyone at once.

"El Paso is a hick cliché insisting that 'the stars at night are big and bright.'"

I controlled my impulse to tell him to go outside and look up.

But he wouldn't have anyway, since he dismissed everything I said and everything the students said. He didn't realize, however, that the kids were too far from New York to be intimidated, and after he muttered to a class, "You just sit there. Say something," one of our most polite students raised her hand. "You're full of shit."

By the night of the awards, the students were so weary of him that when he announced the prizes and stepped from behind the podium to give the winners a hug of congratulation, the first two simply veered around him and left him standing on the stage, staring out at the audience with foolishly extended arms.

Finally a prize winner took pity on him and shook his hand.

But his deflation was already complete.

And it was clear that El Paso had ruined his week, perhaps his year.

Valerie Martin called from Las Cruces, forty-one miles up the freeway from El Paso, to say she'd be teaching at New Mexico State for the year and that I should come by sometime so we could talk about writing.

I remembered her well from the University of New Orleans, where she'd been an undergraduate in English and a student more or less in my circle of classes. I hadn't read the novels she'd published since college, but I did know she had a decent reputation as an author, so my next trip to Las Cruces to see Stephanie, who'd given up her UTEP scholarship to type letters in Mark Medoff's office and earn a degree in his drama department, I stopped at Valerie's office.

The first thing she said was, "You won the Iowa Fiction Award, didn't you?"

I nodded. She looked exactly the same, blond hair over a nervous, intense face, not a month older than the last time I'd seen her in New Orleans.

The second thing she said was, "Do you remember that we screwed the same guys back at UNO? Ronnie and Rich. Ronnie's as handsome as ever with all that curly black hair and those blue eyes, but Rich got so fat you wouldn't recognize him."

"What a shame. He was always so aware of his boxer's physique."

"And so full of himself."

I nodded again. "I haven't been able to find a way to use him in a story yet."

"Me neither."

Which was the total of what we said about writing.

Les probably wore the students out with celebrity, and by the time he brought in Harry Crews, the creative writing classes were jaded.

Crews didn't alienate anyone immediately since the night before he'd staggered drunkenly from a cantina fight into the arms of the El Paso police and had missed the faculty luncheon while he'd been locked up in the El Paso Detention Center. And when he finally got to campus—in time for his afternoon lecture—he said enough valid things about truth and a writer's need to care that the faculty and students forgave the drunken lapse.

He did insist—with a writer's need to stretch the truth and claim humble beginnings—that he was a sharecropper's son, but no one objected to that.

In the auditorium, however, when he read flippant essays about "cancer of the ace" and his vasectomy that supposedly enraged scores of women—including the hospital nurses—because it removed his genes from the pool, the audience wandered out in droves.

Steve, sitting next to Duane and me, had anticipated meeting Crews all semester ("I've read everything he's written, Dr. Carr. He may be my all-time favorite author."), and he listened in glum silence.

The next day, he came to my office with a forlorn face. "I was mistaken. I thought Harry Crews was one of the best."

"Don't feel bad," I said. "I suspect most authors should stay put on the page."

Tony Stafford, as departmental chairman, assigned me an honors class, saying, "You can choose what you want to teach." And, since—surprisingly—he handed me the course a semester ahead of time, I could pick something I wanted to research.

So I decided on Native American literature, which let me read through the library shelves at UTEP, New Mexico State, and the University of New Mexico to combine Native American authors, Southwest history, anthropology, and archaeology.

About the time I reached Native American mythology, I came across a self-published paperback on Mimbres pottery. Although the photographs were grainy and amateurish and the pages badly printed, I had no trouble recognizing the typical black-on-white cartoon men, women, and animals, the exquisite black-and-white geometrics.

One photograph showed four human figures circling a bowl interior, obviously crawling upward with prayer sticks, and other photographs showed bowls with unmistakable images of the humped-back Flute Player. In some bowls Kokopelli wore sunburst earrings and held a prayer stick, sometimes he carried seeds and his flute, and as I sat flipping from one picture to the next, I suddenly recognized that the bowls were telling stories. The illustrations I was seeing were depicting the Pueblo myth of the Emergence, in which the People followed the Flute Player upward through dark underworlds (four or five, depending on the tribe recounting the myth) to reach our present world and emerge from the Sipapu into the sunlight.

And I realized that if those particular bowls narrated Pueblo tales, other Mimbres bowls had to contain native myths as well.

I began reexamining Mimbres Classic pottery for stories.

I rationalized that since we can identify Dionysus on a Greek kylix because we have his description in Homeric texts, I could work backward to do the same. Frank Cushing and other anthropologists had recorded Pueblo myths in the early 1800s before the tales became too contaminated by the white world, so all I had to do was read recorded narratives, examine and sketch as much figured pottery as possible, and then identify the mythic characters and their exploits pictured in the thousand-year-old bowls.

When a bibliography pointed me toward the Los Angeles Museum of History, I wrote to explain my project to the curator and ask if I could fly out to study his collection. He wrote back with a flat "No." He said he intended to write on the museum's Mimbres collection (His project, of course, had nothing to do with mine.) and that I could wait to buy his book to see photographs of the bowls.

I was stunned. I'd told colleagues who refused to discuss authors with me in case I might steal their theories that if they had only one idea, they probably should protect it. But I hadn't expected that kind of protectionism from a museum director.

Without the L.A. collection, I nonetheless found enough pottery to verify twenty or so stories—from The Little War Twins to Spider Woman and the Flood. When I gave the manuscript to Texas Western Press and they sent it out for review, it luckily landed on the desk of art historian J. J. Brody, who said that while he might not agree with the idea of "story bowls," the concept was worth discussing, so he recommended publication.

Which is how scholarship should work.

Les usually didn't have much luck making his famous authors palatable to the students, but the one time he had a real success was when he brought to his awards evening the suave and gentlemanly George Garrett.

George was a friend of Dickey's who'd also taught at Rice and then gone on to the University of Virginia. He told how Jim loved being recognized as the Southern sheriff in the film of his *Deliverance*. "He also likes to be mistaken for a country singer."

"I remember he did play bad guitar every chance he got."

"Did you know Maxine died?"

I nodded. "I saw an obituary in *Time*, but they didn't even mention her name. They just called her 'James Dickey's wife.'"

He shook his head sympathetically, and after a moment, "He's remarried."

I'd heard that and also that the new wife—who might be "Miss Hannah"—was a bit loony, but George was too much of a gentleman to mention that.

He was equally gentlemanly to the students, and the night he passed out the prizes of the by-then-annual literary contest, the students responded by hugging *him*.

When the awards had been bestowed, he gave the novice writers another piece of advice, which I considered as important a message as they'd probably ever get: "Whether you got a second or a third or the one-hundred-dollar first prize tonight, you'll never be more triumphant than you are right now. This is the best it gets. No matter what else you win, you'll never be more successful than you are at this moment."

When the construction worker Doug Gilb confessed that he had a master's degree in philosophy from Santa Barbara—with a specialty in Sanskrit—I wasn't surprised. But I said that since his stories featured mixed cultures ("You told me your mother was from Mexico and your father was German American.") and Latino workers, he should capitalize on the fact that he was one of them. "You don't even have to make anything up. You were there."

"I don't want to be known as a Hispanic writer. I want to be known as a writer."

"I know. I feel the same about being known as a woman writer. But since getting published is the aim, if I were you, I'd emphasize the Latino connection."

I don't know if he paid attention to me or if he came to the same conclusion on his own, but when he sent off to *The Threepenny Review* one of those stories he'd shown Ray Carver and me, he used the Spanish version of his name, "Dagoberto Gilb," and Wendy Lesser took the story.

I think Doug had a quality of innocence that made people—particularly women—want to protect and promote him, and from that first publication, his work was accepted not only by Cinco Puntos Press, a small press run by Lee and Bobby Byrd, but also by the University of New Mexico Press, then Grove, and finally—when his name was recognizable enough—*The New Yorker*. He also won nearly every prize in the literary galaxy, from the Hemingway Award to an NEA to a Guggenheim to being a finalist in the PEN/ Faulkner Awards.

He became furious if someone inferred that his name made any difference, however, so I carefully never brought that up.

Riding up the escalator in the L.A. airport I glanced at a blond young man coming down. As our eyes met, he reached over and held out a paperback to me.

I was too startled not to take the book, but when I got to the top and looked at the title, *The Bhagavad Gita,* I wondered why the kid hadn't just put the paperback down somewhere as I did before I boarded my plane.

About a week later Duane and I stopped off in Washington, D.C., on our way to a conference, and I saw a young black man standing before the Lincoln Memorial, passing out buttons from a huge wicker basket. The buttons read, "I ♥ DC."

"Hey, those are your initials." I walked across the stone paving to get one.

The young man stared at me a second before he reached deep into his basket, brought up a cellophane-wrapped, leather-bound book, and silently held it out.

I looked at the gold embossed title. *The Bhagavad Gita.* Again.

Since Duane read aloud to me while I drove, I gave him the heavy book, and as we cleared the D.C. freeway exits, he started with the opening "Dharma."

In the interminable spiritual battles, conch shells trumpeted, flight after flight of arrows clouded the sky, chariots drawn by splendid white chargers clashed, and not until deep in the text did I hear the sentence, "Success and failure are the same."

"Wait," I said. "Read that again. Success and failure are the same?"

Was a writer a success if he published a book? Did a bad review mean failure? Was she successful if *The New Yorker* took a story? Was she a failure if they didn't?

That was obviously the billboard sentence I'd needed to hear.

The full professors in the department voted me down for professor.

It didn't seem to matter that by then I had more publications than any of them. "You should be older to be a full professor," Tony, ten years my junior, said. But another colleague told me that when the recommendation got to the university president, he said, "Pat Carr is a star in this university," and overturned the rejection.

But then an unforeseen incident occurred.

I'd been elected vice president of the faculty council, and as such I'd been asked to recommend which committees could be eliminated to cut down on bureaucracy. I'd found that at least half a dozen committees duplicated each other or overstepped the bounds they could enforce (such as the grounds committee, which had no control over the grounds crew hired by the university), but since faculty members made points by doing committee work—which in turn influenced their salaries—no one was willing to let his or her committee go.

I tried to tell the faculty senate that if they skipped the bogus meetings, they might be able to publish and not perish, but no one was interested in that advice.

I was in the spotlight, however, and when a retreat was scheduled, I was asked to report on the state of the university. Since I thought the university was doing just fine, I figured I could compliment various departments and sit down.

"You'll have half an hour."

"Half an hour!"

That meant I'd have to do extensive research.

In the meantime, John West had asked me to accept as a correspondence student one of the basketball stars we'd seen when we were both single.

"He lacks only one course to graduate. He's on a professional team and he'll never have to do anything but play basketball, so he'll never need a diploma. But he'd like a degree from the University of Texas at El Paso, and the registrar and the president would like to give him one."

"Of course I'll take him. And since it's correspondence, I can let him write four papers rather than have to come back to take exams."

The basketball player sent two papers, and at the end of the semester, I gave him the usual I for "Incomplete."

"But he can get a grade and the diploma as soon as he sends the other two papers. I won't set a time limit," I said to the registrar, who nodded gravely.

At that point, the academic vice president asked me to speak at the retreat on the state of the university, and I began my research.

As I examined the various colleges and the various majors—and particularly the sports program—I discovered under the coach's rug attempted rapes, dropped felony charges, and gun violations.

And just as suddenly, I discovered an inked C in place of the I I'd penciled into the erstwhile basketball-student's record.

At the retreat I gave the thirty-minute speech on everything I'd uncovered, then concluded with the statement, "I think the university may be in trouble."

The department chairmen sat mute and shocked, and only five of them could bring themselves to applaud. As I left the auditorium, the university vice president caught up with me and said grimly, "This school is not in trouble, Pat."

But other faculty members began leaving cryptic messages on my answering machine that hinted at even more abuses than I'd discovered. The faculty chose sides; everyone made speeches; Les delivered his standard Pogo line, "We have met the enemy and he is us"; townspeople and *The El Paso Times* got involved. Some sports fans defended the coaches, who did their best for the team's black players; others exposed the fact that few of those imported black players graduated or even learned to read at UTEP.

John asked, "Couldn't you have forgotten that you changed that I to a C?"

"No."

The papers reported story after story on the incident, and as I walked across campus one afternoon, a man—obviously a fellow faculty member but someone I didn't know—murmured, "So you're the little lady who's bringing down the university."

Finally, a special committee, convened to debate the faked grade and the faked diploma, decided that since the latter had been awarded, everyone should let the black player graduate and just drop the whole matter.

But it was too late. The administration collapsed.

The registrar, the vice president, and the president were forced to resign.

And then another unfortunate event occurred.

Before I'd discovered Duane, the Political Science Department had discovered vacation land in New Mexico selling for next to nothing, and one afternoon at the Kern Place Tavern, Howard, building a vacation home there, suggested I go look at it.

Paul said he'd drive me up. "You're a compulsive buyer, but I'll keep you from buying a godforsaken piece of desert just because some lover's got a house there."

Our salesman showed us Howard's unfinished cabin before he stopped at a nearby four-acre plot covered with piñon pines and scrub oak. Across green valleys, snow-topped blue mountains rose into a crystal sky, and Paul caught his breath. "This is beautiful! It's just five hundred dollars down. Buy it! You can afford it! You have to buy it!"

And when amid the turmoil on campus I found a tumor in my thigh (My mother had lived two years after the discovery of her first tumor.), I decided I didn't want to spend the final two years of my life at the uneasy university I'd helped fracture. We could leave academia and live off our savings.

We could never afford New York, but since I already owned four acres in New Mexico, I remembered that factory-made houses could be dragged into the mountains and their two halves put together over a weekend.

The manager of the New Mexico land project was ecstatic. He needed homes to rent to salesmen who lived and sold acreage in the vacation town called Timberon, and he eagerly found us a great buy on a module. So we didn't tell him we had no intention of renting out our hideaway, that we were going to sit in it and write for two years.

Honey had always loved our huge stucco house in Kern Place—a few blocks from the tavern—and since my father had died and she'd received her Ph.D. from the University of Houston (with a dissertation on John Rechy), there was nothing to keep her close to Houston. So she and Tom bought the house from us and moved to El Paso.

Duane and I boxed up the novels we might read again, gave away the remaining books in our wall-to-wall basement bookcases, and unloaded in garage sales the furniture too large for small module rooms. We took Maximilian's bed, Ken's chair, the red velvet Federal love seat, my 1810 silver tea set, and the artifacts. Stephanie and Shelley were both in college—Stephanie a junior at New Mexico State, still working in Mark Medoff's office, and Shelley starting at Texas Tech—so Sean and Jennifer each had a bedroom.

Since we'd be living for two years on a limited budget, we returned the propane tank and outfitted the house for wood with a Franklin stove in the living room, a wood cookstove in the kitchen, and a wood-burning water heater in the tiny laundry room. We lived three miles from the lodge and meager grocery/post office, where the school bus stopped to take Timberon children to a country school in Weed, and we reveled in our isolation. On our hilltop across the valley from the blue mountains, we planted fruits and vegetables advertised to produce the first spring: asparagus, strawberries, grapes, and one huge, accidental pumpkin whose seed had somehow landed in the grape arbor.

And as I wrote, I watched the vines blossom and the fruit plump through the summer in the exquisitely beautiful place where I planned to spend my last two years.

The tiny town of Weed lay an hour and a half by bus from Timberon, so during the three coldest months of the year, the resident salesmen decided to petition the school board to give the fourteen Timberon elementary children their own school rather than have them make that snow-packed round-trip journey every day. By then the residents had realized that Duane and I had Ph.D.s, so they asked if we'd teach for those months.

We knew no one else was qualified, and when the school board in Alamagordo agreed to the plan, we felt we had to agree as well—"It's just for three months." So we drove down the winding hill road to Alamogordo to see the superintendent.

He nodded the pompous nod school superintendents use for teachers and parents. "We'll have two classes, kindergarten, first, and second, then third through sixth." He looked at me. "You'll take the younger children. Your husband will take the older ones."

It was such a blatantly chauvinistic comment that I said at once, "No, I'll take the older ones and he'll take the little guys." (Duane later confessed that he'd never had so much fun teaching as he had with kindergarten, first, and second graders.)

The school board allocated the funds to drag in a module and modify it into one large classroom (Duane and I—with half a dozen volunteers—painted the exterior red so the kids could have the joint experience of a little red schoolhouse and a one-room school.) and set aside enough money to pay us and an aide, Sharon Carter, one of the salesmen's wives. A high school dropout, Sharon took the GED so she could work at the only school in New Mexico whose teachers all had Ph.D.s.

When I had told John I intended to marry Duane, he'd asked me to be kind. So when I wrote "An El Paso Idyll," I did try to be kind.

I wrote the characters as being in love. But I created a male too rooted in Texas prescriptive rules to get the woman he wants, and when he loses her, he has to erase her from his life by destroying her career. I tried to emphasize his confused and—what I considered tragic—conflict by naming the character "Willie," after Willy Loman in *Death of a Salesman*, and "Leer," after *King Lear*.

Too many editors sent back the story with such comments as, "He certainly is a leering son of a bitch, isn't he?" So I finally renamed him "Willie Oaks"—after Gabriel Oaks in one of those Hardy novels Dr. McKillop at Rice had loved. As soon as I made the name change, the editor at *The Seattle Review* took the story.

I couldn't alter the character enough, however (Perhaps no author can.), and my UTEP colleagues said the second they read the reprinted story in an anthology of Texas women writers, they recognized the model. My friend Mimi said she raced down the hall of the English building shouting, "Look at this!"

I never solicited comments from anyone else in the department, but once when I went to UTEP to give a reading, a former colleague asked, "Are you going to read *the* story?"

The story!

I felt as if I'd just won an Oscar.

When I give workshops, women writers almost always ask how my writer husband reacts to the fact that I'm more successful than he is.

"Men are competitive, Dr. Carr, and especially since you're both writers, you must have to be careful when you get something published."

"The man I'm married to is just not competitive. But since he writes from the male point of view and I write from the female perspective, there's no way we could compete anyway. He can't write what I write. I can't—and have no intention of—writing what he does. When he gets a sonnet or a song published or I get a story published, we buy a bottle of champagne and celebrate. I may be wrong, but I've never seen a hint that we're not feeling the same pride in each other's work that we feel in our own."

At least a few of them always look at me dubiously, and finally someone—usually a woman who grew up in the '50s—will ask, "You have a lot of stories about affairs. How does he handle that?"

I don't quite know how to explain that he's too confident even to consider "handling" it, that he approves the successes of anyone he knows I slept with—"They didn't get you, so they may as well have something"—and that once he said, "If you thought anyone else was better in bed than I am, you'd be with him." So I usually say, "A writer can make one birth, one affair, one dead body do for dozens of stories. Besides, all my affairs occurred when I was married to someone else."

Two years in Timberon abruptly passed and I was still alive.

Despite our lovely hilltop, the vacation lots were being diced smaller and smaller, and our once-isolated escape grew more and more crowded. So I found Sean's United Farm catalogue to see if, like Huckleberry Finn, we should move farther from civilization. As I picked up the catalogue to check "Arizona," it fell open to "Arkansas."

"Duane Carr, come look at these prices. We could buy twice as much land there."

We drove to Arkansas, and the United Farm agent showed us houses and land. One thirty-acre piece, nestled against a hundred-foot bluff, had an exquisite view of the violet Boston Mountains rising across lush pastures, thick stands of cedars, and the White River. The house had new plumbing, but it also had broken porch boards, a dirt yard littered with shattered doors, rotting clothes, and rusting bedsprings. The tongue-and-groove oak slats had been painted orange in the kitchen and bile green in the hall.

"A real estate agent bought it for a hunting cabin, but he made some bad investments and he wants to sell. It's got a million-dollar view, but it's only thirty-five thousand."

I knew Americans hated to bargain. "Will he take twenty-five thousand?"

His eyes glittered as he said, "I'll see," and I could tell they were hardly friends.

An hour later when I asked, "Should we call back and offer thirty thousand for that view?" he shook his head. "We'll wait one more hour."

Before the hour passed, the other real estate agent slouched up the sidewalk and accepted twenty-five thousand dollars for his mountain cabin.

And suddenly we owned thirty acres of Arkansas and a million-dollar view.

In Dublin, I'd deemed Ireland in January the coldest place on earth, but now I realized northwest Arkansas was. In my Wyoming childhood, winter days routinely hit minus 40°, but as sunlight sparkled on frozen ice, the walls of the snow paths, shoveled by my father through the drifts, had towered—warm as igloos—over our snowsuits. In January Arkansas, however, while we worked on the shack we'd bought, the wind rarely stopped. It moaned against the windows, rattled the clapboards, swirled dirt up from the pilings through the floor to layer the cold moist tongue-and-groove bead-board with icy grit.

We didn't try to salvage the stained refrigerator, the yellow metal sink—skirted with cotton print curtains to hide the pipes—or the chartreuse shag rug. After Duane dismantled shelves someone had built over the old-fashioned windows so light could penetrate the rooms, he started replacing porch boards before someone stepped out the front door and dropped through. I bricked up a firewall so the wood stove we planned to buy wouldn't set fire to the ancient oak timbers.

The afternoon we found a stove at a hardware store in Farmington, however, I realized Arkansas had another distinctive quality besides high-humidity chill.

Duane took out his credit card, but the owner shifted a tobacco plug to his other cheek and held up a hand with veins as thick as earthworms. "I don't take plastic."

"We haven't brought a checkbook. But we can drive back in an hour or so."

"Naw." He had no more than glanced at us, and now he merely studied the economy-sized pork-and-bean can that was his spittoon. "I trust you. Go ahead and take the stove. You can send me a check."

The Elkins school district called to say that Jennifer
was too advanced for fourth grade. "Can we put her in
fifth?" I didn't know if that was a good idea since my father
had refused to allow Wyoming schools to skip me, but we
decided being younger might be better than being bored.
So we let her move ahead.

She'd always wanted a horse, and to keep her occupied
after school while we labored on the house, I called the
number in a *Star Shopper* ad for a Welsh pony. "What do you
think, Duane Carr? They're only asking a hundred dollars."

We traveled one back road after another until at last,
deep in the hills, in a dirt cul-de-sac, we found a compound
that spewed forth half a dozen young women, lots of tum-
bling children, two young men, and an older man, obviously the one in charge. He introduced himself as "Shepherd."

He wore shoulder-length hair, a long brown beard, and
sandals with jeans and plaid wool shirt, but I managed not
to ask if he'd actually said, "*The* Shepherd."

"Horses are social." He led us to a sweet-faced white
mare and a brown stallion with a creamy mane and tail.
Both ponies flicked their tails and eyed us. "They're happier
if they have company. I can let you have the two of them
for one fifty."

We didn't know horses, but we'd both read *Swift*, and
the sociability sounded logical, so we wrote the check, and
Shepherd said, "I'll bring 'em over Monday."

When he came, however, the horse trailer carried the
two ponies and a tall ("She's fourteen hands.") strawberry
roan. "She'll get too lonely by herself. Take her for free."

So Jennifer—and we—abruptly owned three sociable
horses.

When the wind did finally slack and sleet encased black elm limbs in thin tubes of crystal as calm and transparent as polished glass, nothing seemed truer than the pale morning sun topping the bluff and spreading like oil across the frozen pasture. And nothing glittered more brilliantly than the ice sculptures of sheathed amber weeds beside the gravel road. In the spring, as blooms dropped from bead-sized nubs of peaches, pears, and cherries, new leaves unfurled to shelter the house in a vast basket of romaine green and flickering sun.

Cedars and hardwoods had met in this swath of Arkansas, along with roadrunners and armadillos and squirrels, to merge the West and the South. Every kind of poisonous snake existed on our land—from rattlers to cottonmouths to corals and water moccasins—with every kind of insect, tarantula, and scorpion, and during the summer I could track the life cycles of ticks and butterflies. In the fall, almonds, chestnuts, black walnuts, and hickory nuts littered the ground, and in the winter, vermilion persimmons ripened after the first hard freeze.

Once when I gave a reading in Evansville, Indiana, I was introduced by a professor who noted that his faculty knew my work, that five of my ex-students sat in the audience, that the evening had the feel of a reunion even though I'd never been in Evansville before. Then he added, "We all know you can't go home again, but maybe you can go home for the first time."

I'd had to forgo New York and my beloved El Paso. But at least I'd relinquished them to go home for the first time to the Garden of Eden.

One afternoon Shepherd drove up with two dogs
in his truck bed. Mottled black-gray Australian sheepdogs
with one blue and one brown eye, they were the ugliest
dogs I'd ever seen. Shepherd asked if we could keep them
while he fought for his children. "We figured to home
school them, but the state come and took them away."

When we expressed our sympathy, he asked if we'd
give a deposition to his lawyer about how we'd seen their
spotless houses, their tote bags of nutritious rice and beans,
their pantry sparkling with jars of canned carrots and poke
greens. "Don't swear to what you don't know, just to what
you seen. I'd sure appreciate your help."

We agreed, and when the lawyer called, we drove to
Fayetteville, sat in a courthouse chamber, and testified to
a court reporter. "The kids have long hair, but it's freshly
shampooed. There *are* more mothers than fathers, but
Mormons have that imbalance, too." We mentioned the
hard-swept floors, hard-scrubbed windows. Since some
of Jennifer's teachers—and the lawyer himself—made the
same fierce grammatical errors, I didn't mention my hesita-
tions about the quality of Shepherd's home schooling, and
a couple of days later, the lawyer phoned to thank us. Our
testimony had convinced the judge to let Shepherd keep
the children. "Y'all have the credentials."

But a week after that he called with news that Shepherd's commune had vanished. "They up and left the state.
That don't imply guilt about the sexual abuse charges,
but—"

"Sexual abuse charges!"

"Didn't I mention that? We'll probably never know for
sure, of course."

We did know for sure that no one ever came for the
homely Australian shepherds.

Hillary and Bill Clinton occupied the governor's mansion at the time, and I went to a university luncheon to hear Hillary speak. I sat with her good friend, Ellen Gilchrist, while the First Lady of Arkansas spoke of women's issues and lamented that so few women wrote the female experience. After the luncheon, I went to the head table and said I happened to have a collection of short stories on women's experiences. "I'll send a copy of my *Women in the Mirror* down to you."

Two weeks later, Jennifer brought home Hillary's reply.

Jennifer walked the mile home with the mail every school day after she got off the bus, but that day, a Saturday, she'd picked up the letters while out riding with Judy Gabbard, a woman who lived on the next hill and worked in the Levi's plant.

Judy liked to ride and to read, and when Jennifer told her I wrote, she'd asked to see one of my books. As their horses cantered up, I noticed Judy carried the copy of *The Women in the Mirror* Jennifer had loaned her.

She studied me while she slid down from the saddle and handed me the book. "You really visited those places you wrote about, didn't you?"

I nodded.

Then Jennifer gave me the stack of mail containing Hillary Clinton's note that said, "Your stories are extraordinary. I hesitated for a minute over the word to use because they provoked such different responses and emotions in me. 'The Party' has stayed with me like a knot in my gut since I read it."

I couldn't decide which comment I valued more.

In *The Arkansas Gazette* **I saw a six-line ad** about a group calling itself the International Women's Writing Guild. The group would hold a conference in June in Saratoga Springs, New York, that would focus on the general topic of myth. A New York telephone number had been listed.

"You know," I said to Duane. "I think I'd like to do this."

"You sure?"

"You know how I feel about New York. Why don't I just call and see."

When I called, a lilting feminine voice—with as strong a German accent as my grandfather had had—answered the phone. "This is Hannelore Hahn."

When I mentioned the ad and said I had an archaeology monograph on myth, *Mimbres Mythology*, and that my collection of original myths, *Sonahchi*, based on the anthropological ones, had come out with Cinco Puntos Press, she said all the conference teaching slots had been assigned but that she could pay me fifty dollars to give a ten-minute presentation on Saturday. "You'll get a room and meals on Friday and Saturday."

I said I'd come.

As I stood in Grand Central, reading the board for the Adirondack train to Saratoga Springs, a dainty five-foot blonde clicked up beside me in tiny heels. She stopped and looked hard at me. In a heavy German accent, she said, "You're Pat Carr?"

We'd had one telephone conversation. I hadn't opened my mouth in the station, and I was dressed in the typical black jeans and black sweater of a New Yorker.

So, of course, I was instantly hooked.

But on the three-hour train ride to Saratoga Springs, I wondered what I'd let myself in for.

I might be more my sister's keeper than my brother's, but I didn't know females. I'd missed them completely in elementary school, in high school I'd taken college-track courses, which contained mainly boys, and while the Rice student population boasted that eight-to-one male-female ratio, most classes I took—German, Russian, Logic, Philosophy—had even fewer girls. Although I could claim a few women friends, throughout my teaching career, my peers in the Assistant, Associate, and Full Professor levels had been men. The majority of university women, adjuncts or lecturers, taught freshman English, and it was the males in the department with whom I discussed "serious" literature, with whom I coauthored academic papers.

And here I was traveling to Skidmore College to be with three hundred women.

What would I talk about? I was beyond the marriage, divorce, baby, and maid stages, even the card-playing stage. What could we discuss? Recipes?

What the hell was I doing?

But strangely enough, I found that the women could talk intelligently. Most had published stories, poems, or essays. Some had published books, some had manuscripts under contract, and one said, "My agent is McIntosh & Otis. Why not send a query and mention my name?"

Epiphanies filled the weekend.

At the cocktail party following a reading by a local Fayetteville poet, I stopped at the hors d'oeuvre table beside Jack Butler, a novelist from Little Rock. I spoke first.

"Did you see that Crescent Dragonwagon is offering the prize of a romantic weekend for the story of your most romantic moment? Her father, Maurice Zolotov, is the judge." (Crescent told me she'd decided in her wild hippie days to pick a name that stood out, and while I might not have encouraged that particular fanciful combination, she did at least have the perseverance to stick with it in all her children's books.) "Do you have a most romantic moment, Jack?"

He nodded, and although I never saw his entry, I knew we both sent something.

The winning narrative belonged to an elderly man whose story told how he'd seen his wife, who was then dying of cancer, for the first time when they'd been in the third grade. No ordinary romantic moment could have beaten that. And the next time I saw Jack, I said, "We didn't have a prayer this year. But are you going to enter again?"

He looked shocked. "You have only one *most* romantic moment."

I thought, How like a man, but I didn't say it.

And the following year when I won the contest, Duane and I left Jennifer with my friend Judy and went off for the romantic stay at Crescent's bed-and-breakfast.

I never mentioned to her that I'd met her parents, or that I liked Maurice much better after that weekend than I'd liked him the evening in Colorado when he'd trashed Marilyn Monroe.

Reinvited to the International Women's Writing Guild as a workshop instructor, I flew back to Skidmore College, and this time I introduced my de rigueur topic. Sadly, I discovered that women were as loath as men to give up the cherished idea that a "real" writer can write any experience, from any point of view. I'd assumed women would understand that since men held sway over world literature, women characters had been undervalued for centuries. I assumed they'd know that women authors had to write their females honestly to correct hundreds of years of male-dominated mistakes.

They didn't.

And too many reacted with the same fury I'd encountered in male writers.

Some objected violently; others left the room and refused to make eye contact the rest of the week. One woman who'd worked with Mother Teresa said she couldn't come back to my class because she was getting too angry and wanted to slap upside the head all the women who argued with me.

The women conferees still believed that men had all the fun and all the adventures. Even as I quoted a young male colleague's objection, "If you cut us off from the female point of view, you're cutting us off from all significant experiences," I couldn't get through to them that *any* man knew male perspectives better than they did. I couldn't make them understand they'd remain second-rate—with inauthentic stories based on guesswork—if they continued to write from the male point of view.

But by the end of the week, scores of women still sat in my sessions, and one of them said, "Why don't they just shut up and read your work."

Miller Williams, who hailed from Arkansas himself and who'd become head of the University of Arkansas Press, always welcomed me warmly when I dropped by, and he always read the manuscripts I brought.

He often told me I was the most exciting author he'd read in a long time, and early in 1986 he called to say that he was 90 percent sure he could get a collection of my short stories through the press committee. "Do you have someone who knows your work who could judge the manuscript?"

I'll never be sure if I still luxuriated in the fact that I'd known no one at Iowa when I'd won their prize a decade before, or if deep down I just couldn't stand the thought that my work needed the approval of a kind friend. But whichever it was, I said, "I think I'll go with Fate, Miller. I'm going to let the collection take its chances."

The manuscript came back flatly rejected.

Miller called, and with reluctance in his voice, he said that such an adamant refusal canceled any plan he'd had of presenting my collection to the board of the press.

So I went by the office to pick up the manuscript.

As I trudged back to the car, I wished I'd never heard of Fate. Or of James Dickey.

So I didn't have a short story collection come out with the University of Arkansas Press, but in 1986 I did have two other books appear.

I'd known Pat Littledog at UTEP (As a grad student, she'd also entered the Iowa contest, and the afternoon I won, I stopped by to tell her: "I'm sorry your manuscript didn't win, Pat. But I'd be sorrier if it had."), and when she started Slough Press with Chuck Taylor, they, too, asked if I had anything. I'd written a collection of El Paso stories, and when the press received a Texas Commission on the Arts grant to help with publication, Pat and Chuck brought out *Night of the Luminarias*.

That same year I published the Civil War letters of Ras Stirman, *In Fine Spirits*. The head of the U. of A. library's Special Collections had offered me the box of letters and had asked if I'd be interested in editing them. Ras, a Fayetteville native and the youngest Confederate colonel in the war, had written to his sister Rebecca, and since he rarely mentioned battles and wrote instead about dances, parties, and falling in love, he ended every letter saying that he—and the rest of the boys—were "in fine spirits."

I got an endowment from the Arkansas Humanities Council to work on the edition, and the Washington County Historical Society brought it out when I finished.

Appropriately enough, both Texas and Arkansas had become states in 1836, and both books appeared for their respective state's celebration of 150 years of statehood.

Of course, I don't think anyone—except maybe Duane and me—noticed the books or their dates.

I kept being invited to give summer workshops for the IWWG and I kept insisting that no good writer should write from *inside* a character whose sex, race, age, religion, class, or nationality she hadn't been. And when one woman came up in the cafeteria and asked for my most succinct rationale why women shouldn't write from the male point of view, I said, "Because it's immoral."

She looked a little startled, but she nodded. "Thank you."

One summer, the topic of mothers came up in the sessions more than usual, and most conferees agreed that people had to come to terms with their hatred of their mothers.

I remembered Jack and his mother and his comment that "none of us should ever have been children," while I considered my relationship with my mother.

I knew her self-absorption, her inability to care, and as I sat in classrooms filled with women struggling with dislike of their mothers, I struggled with my own response. Not only had I understood my mother, but I'd loved her. I'd never even challenged her. Would I have responded the same to Josef Mengele if I'd known him?

On Wednesday morning, as I stood in the bathroom putting on mascara, my suite mate, Sister Paula, came in and our eyes met in the mirror. She smiled. "Are you having a good conference?"

I sighed. "I'm mulling over how I felt about my mother. She was the embodiment of indifference, which Shaw says is mankind's worst inhumanity. But I cared about her."

She gave a gentle nun laugh. "No one needs a reason to love. People have to find an excuse only if they hate."

If success and failure were the same, why should I
rage at an editor who misunderstood a story? How could
I write the editor at *The New Yorker*, who said, "All of us up
and down the hall liked this story," and ask why the hell
they hadn't accepted it? Despite my egregious error at the
U. of A. Press, I remained fatalistic, and I still told myself—
with more or less success—that a rejected story wasn't
meant to appear at that time or in that particular literary
magazine. I still glanced at and tossed rejection slips.

Duane often said, "You aren't human. No one can take
the rejection you do." Miller would see me at some literary
event and say, "You're my most spectacular failure. You're
one of the best writers I've run into in years, and I can't get
you published." Even Doug Gilb, when he called with some
new publishing triumph, would say, "How do you do it?
How do you keep writing with no more success than you
have?"

"Well, I have something to say."

"Oh. OK. Go ahead and say it."

"No, Doug, I meant I keep writing because I have something I want to say."

I told classes love was the power that moved the uni-
verse; I told them writers had to care about their characters
and they had to make readers care. I kept saying the only
reason for any author to write was to foster understanding.

Of course I was out of sync with America, with the
world. During 90 percent approval of Bush's Gulf War, who
wanted to hear that we should care about each other?

But I kept writing about love and understanding. And I
hoped that one day, a publisher might ask, as they'd asked
Faulkner, if I had anything else at home.

July 1987, in our small corner of Eden, the underground spring and pond went dry, and in August, Duane and I had to take part-time teaching jobs at the University of Arkansas at Little Rock. After a semester, when the English Department ran out of classes for two part-time adjuncts, we found jobs teaching nursing students at nearby Baptist Hospital.

And for the second time in academia, I did give away a grade.

The first time had been at UTEP during the Vietnam War when a young man with a C had pleaded for a B so he could stay in school and avoid the draft. I'd looked at his peach-fuzz cheeks. "All right. But remember it's a gift. I don't believe in this war, and I don't want it on my conscience that you got killed your first day in Saigon. So I'm *giving* you a B. This time. Earn it next time."

"I won't let you down, Dr. Carr."

At Baptist Hospital, the gift was to an LPN from the burn unit who'd tried for years to pass the course so she could become an RN. An older woman, she couldn't match her verbs to her subjects no matter how hard she tried, but I'd read her journal, and despite the errors, I couldn't miss her concern for the horribly burned. I knew she was the kind of RN I'd want if I were ever hospitalized.

So as the semester ended, I said, "We both know your grammar is still a D, but one of these days, noun and verb agreement will click in your head (I tried hard to believe it.), and you'll see how the language works. So I'm putting a B on your record."

She may not have had any more faith in the miracle than I did, but together we nodded, and she gave me a lopsided smile of gratitude as she went into the hall.

Leslie Ullman, who took over UTEP's creative writing specialty when Les Standiford moved to Florida, invited me to read in El Paso, and when I got there, she ushered me through the English office. As we walked in she saw John. "Oh, my God. There he is."

But John smiled, said, "Hey, you've got some gray in your hair," and I answered, "Don't we all," in a not-very-clever bon mot exchange—as if we'd been brief acquaintances. I guessed *the* story had been kind enough for him.

While we waited in Leslie's office for my reading, she shared one of her newly published poems about a woman's response to rape. When I finished reading it, I asked, "How long did you have to process that? How long ago were you raped?"

"Oh, I haven't been raped. You don't have to be raped to write about it."

I'd always envied my friend Joan, who gave people a flat "No" when she refused an invitation, who often said, "Hell, no," for really sorry invitations.

I sat in Leslie's office and wished I could have told her that her poem was dishonest, that it might actually cause irreparable harm. But somehow I couldn't say that she was an established poet, and since she'd had her rape poem accepted, publishers of literary journals could stop searching for an authentic one. A lesser-known writer might write an honest poem offering insight for rape victims or for rapists, but it might never get out there because her poem, based on other women's trauma, had already been published.

I didn't say anything, but I wished just once I could have been Joan.

I saw in the *Chronicle of Higher Education* that the University of New Orleans might be funding instructorships—full time, four classes each—at eighteen thousand dollars a year. The department chairman was my friend and fellow Tulane Ph.D., Malcolm Magaw, so Duane and I immediately sent off application letters.

Malcolm wrote back saying it would be an insult to offer an instructorship with such a low salary to teachers of our caliber.

We were still out of water on our land, we still needed the jobs and the pittance they paid, and I wanted to write and ask him to insult us, but I didn't. His kind letter was a rejection, and I always let them stand.

But two weeks later, the secretary of the UNO English Department called to say that the instructorships had been funded. She added that Dr. Magaw was out of town, but since she'd typed a personal letter from him to me and thus knew I was an old friend whom he'd want to hire, she was offering us two of the jobs.

I accepted for us instantly.

Jennifer had found her best friend Jeannie in Little Rock and wanted to stay at Central High. We couldn't turn down such a fated offer, but since Stephanie had just returned from Hawaii and was willing to chaperone Jennifer in Little Rock, we rented them an apartment and drove to New Orleans.

We found a little place on Robert E. Lee, within walking distance of Lake Pontchartrain and the university, and finally I began teaching full time at UNO.

When our lease was up on Robert E. Lee, we decided that since we didn't have to send a child to school down Bourbon Street—we had with us only a little Sheltie named Faulkner—we could rent in the French Quarter. We found a tiny converted slave quarter on Royal, above a patio restaurant and opposite the antebellum wrought-iron cornstalk fence I'd once pointed out on literary tours, and we immediately discovered that the Vieux Carré was the safest place in the city.

Streetlights and neon flickered on at dusk and lit the packed streets until dawn. Someone always stood talking or laughing below the balconies, and at three in the morning, the soothing clop of the horse-drawn carriages sounded from the brick streets. No one seemed to mind the garbage on the curbs—often crowned with antique sewing rockers or oil paintings left for some Quarter dweller to find and use—and no one frowned on bizarre behavior or objected to Duane taking Faulkner on his evening walk through the patio restaurant. No one said a word as the little dog eyed the diners with disdain and wagged his tail past their shrimp cocktails and bread puddings.

When we spent Mardi Gras in the Quarter and attended the seven-in-the-morning Zulu Parade, I also discovered that the Southern gentleman who'd disappeared from literature was alive and well in the black Mardi Gras celebrants. When I'd lived in New Orleans before and had stood on Canal to watch Rex paraders toss plastic necklaces and fake coins to a white crowd, I'd seen men stamp on fingers reaching for a coin and elbow children aside for a string of beads. But on Rampart, both men and women would catch a throw, turn to us, and ask, "You have one of these? I got one already."

Malcolm said, "I see you two walking to campus, holding hands, your faces turned toward each other as you talk." He smiled. "It must be nice to be that in love."

New Orleans was probably *the* place to be in love. Talking to someone who listened, stopping at the Café du Monde for café au lait, or hearing from the Madelaine the nine-year-old trumpeter in Jackson Square imitating Louis Armstrong.

But as much as I loved being in love in New Orleans, UNO was cheating its students. The dean was using Freshman English to weed them out, and no matter what grade they earned in class, they either passed or failed the semester on the faculty-graded score of an exit exam.

Freshman English teachers sat in their offices in despair, and while I saw it as a question of academic freedom, I didn't have the energy to make the fight—again.

So when an old friend from Tulsa University called to say that his department at Western Kentucky University had an opening for an assistant professor and asked if I'd be interested, I took the interview.

As we drove to Bowling Green, Kentucky, Duane said, "No one gives up a full professorship and starts over as an assistant professor."

But since lead times for promotion and tenure were waived, I became an associate professor within a couple of years, and a full professor soon after.

Duane said, "You ought to be in the Guinness Book of Records."

The first year at Western Kentucky, I led eighteen students to Ireland and finally got to teach the writers of my specialty: Yeats, Joyce, O'Faolain, Synge, Friel, O'Connor. We trekked through Dublin and Galway to see sites of the 1916 Rebellion; we climbed Yeats's and Joyce's towers, walked around Howth, and collected stones on the beaches of the Irish Sea. Irish scholars came to explain "The Troubles," and Joyce's nephew read from *Finnegan's Wake* with a beautiful Irish accent that made the puns almost meaningful. We also managed to get tickets to *Juno and the Paycock* at the Abbey Theatre.

Redone in glittering gilt and red velvet, the refurbished Abbey had sold out. Standing room overflowed, and, ignoring Dublin's fire marshal, three or four people perched on every aisle step. The production was heart-stopping, and when the actor playing Joxer accidentally missed an exit door and slammed into a wall, he recovered so quickly and so authentically that the audience thought the crash had been rehearsed. At intermission, when I went down front to see how my students responded to the first act, they looked at me smiling, and one of them asked, "Do you have a seat belt back there where you're sitting, Dr. Carr?"

Duane agreed he'd never seen me so high, and after the final curtain when we emerged from the theater, caught a cab, and heard the driver say, "I hope you liked the play. O'Casey is one of our own, you know," I knew that my favorite author had at last found appreciation in his hometown.

I felt that my little Irish father, with that possible royal "O" before his name, had somehow been justified, too.

I kept giving classes for the IWWG, and Hannelore kept finding surprisingly good writers to lead her workshops. The first time I met Barbara Kingsolver was at a Guild conference in Santa Fe. A third presenter didn't show, and when a harried Hannelore had the empty slot to fill, I suggested to Barbara that we take over and discuss writing. By then I had more than enough practice keeping conversations flowing, and Hannelore was so impressed that she suggested we give joint workshops for the Guild. We were naturally invited to Skidmore College that summer.

Since Barbara had just had great success with *The Bean Trees*, a host of women came to hear her, and when I suggested we do joint evening critique sessions, we again worked so well together that scores of women brought in their manuscripts.

Barbara was revising *Animal Dreams*, and at the end of the week, she gave me the manuscript to see if she'd done a good enough job with Henry's interior thoughts.

I wrote back that I'd be happier if she changed Henry to Henrietta.

She answered that she was examining "motherlessness" and needed a father character, so I didn't say that since both her parents were still alive, motherlessness was not much more honest than the male point of view.

Animal Dreams came out with Henry still in the plot, and when her short story collection also appeared and contained a story with a male point of view, she asked if she'd written the story and the novel to my satisfaction.

Since it was a direct question I had to say that at least she hadn't done too much harm.

Barbara was the college roommate I'd never had. We shared shampoo and the hours after midnight when we both woke up with insomnia, and she said we probably should form an insomniacs' club that would hold meetings in the darkness of 3:00 a.m. Since we were always awake by breakfast, we usually stood first in line at the college cafeteria, and the first morning, she nudged me. "Look, Pat, they have grits."

"Sorry, Barbara, we're in New York. That's Cream of Wheat."

We laughed at the same foibles, we agreed on the same values in literature, and we both harbored the same politics, so it didn't surprise me too much to have a number of Skidmore conferees come up during the week and say that not only did our critiques sound alike but that our styles were similar.

I didn't envy Barbara's writing, and I knew that with our twenty-five-year age gap, with her Kentucky background of a doctor father and my Wyoming camp boss father, we couldn't really write the same stories. I said constantly— and tried hard to believe it—that literature needs us all, and the only time I can remember being envious of anyone else's narrative was when I'd read the opening description of El Paso in John Rechy's *City of Night*. I'd sat on my third-floor Cali balcony, overlooking the huge avocado tree with its green fruit the size and shape of green lightbulbs, and wished I'd written that passage.

So I didn't want to have written any of Barbara's words, but I did realize I was a bit envious of her fabulous success.

During a July school break I sprained my wrist sawing wood.

Since I'd never read much George Eliot, I decided to run through her entire body of work while my wrist healed. And when I got to *Middlemarch*, I knew the novel I had to write: five American women in Cali during the 1960s when the *violencia* was at its height, each woman dealing with her own version of love and the "Colombian adventure" as she languishes beneath the hill with its three askew crosses.

As I wrote, I felt each episode bleed seamlessly into the next, and I finished the novel in six weeks. I sent it off, and my agent wrote back that she loved it and would try a new small publisher, Permanent Press.

A couple of weeks later, the Permanent Press editor called to say that he'd read a hundred pages and that if the rest of the novel was as good as those, he definitely wanted to publish it. I assured him the rest of the novel was as good.

But in the next mail, I got the manuscript back, accompanied by a form rejection.

That was the one rejection slip I should have called about. I didn't.

But *Beneath the Hill* is still the one novel I can read as if someone else had written it. I said in it all I wanted to say about love—five different versions of my favorite topic in the right points of view—and I rarely even find typos in the pages when I go back to the copy that came out later with another small press.

Nonetheless, I'll always be grateful to the women at IWWG conferences who buy the book and the ones who said, "I read your novel. It's a masterpiece."

On one trip to Saratoga Springs I didn't fly but took the bus to Washington and then on to New York, just as I had after high school graduation.

This time the bus, scheduled to reach the city after midnight, carried all black passengers. When we reached the Port Authority, we unloaded and wished each other good luck, then I hurried upstairs to the Adirondack counter to catch my final bus.

The ticket master had begun closing his counter as I reached him. "I'd like a ticket on the next bus to Saratoga Springs."

He locked the chain-link gate in place. "Come back at seven tomorrow morning."

"No, I meant the *next* bus."

"That's the next bus." He walked away.

I realized the whole place was empty and every counter eerily locked.

I went back downstairs where I'd left my fellow passengers and discovered they'd been equally marooned. Since the homeless occupied every seat in the lobby, those of us from the bus spent the night sharing floor space and the sleeping bags two kids had brought. We watched the police hassle a black kid lying with his head in the lap of a red-haired, freckled girl ("Don't get involved, Pat. Don't make more trouble for him."), and we partnered to the rest room since rapes occurred nightly in the stalls.

When I wrote about that night and sent the story to a midwestern journal, the editor called it "too sensational" to print.

The editor at *The New Yorker* called it "too ordinary" to accept. "You're just giving us a slice of life."

In the mid-'90s Bob Gover came briefly back into my life.

I'd given a workshop in Little Rock where Kirk Polking, head of the Writer's Digest School, was also on the program, and a couple of years later when she retired, the school asked me to come to Cincinnati to see if I'd like to take over the directorship.

I read that Gover was on their faculty, and I called the number in the brochure.

He sounded exactly as he had the last time I'd heard him decades before, and when I told him I was considering the Writer's Digest School, he said, "I wish you'd take it. They're trying to get rid of me, and I'd have an in if you were head."

It seemed that Genelle had taken him for everything, even the mansion in Santa Barbara, and though his wife (technically his second, I guess) was a psychologist or psychiatrist, they didn't have a decent income. As he talked, I thought what a sad commentary on fame. And on all his Monopoly money. The school paid five dollars for the initial assignments, adding a few dollars while the pupil remained with the program, until at last, the instructor could earn as much as twelve dollars for the final revision.

"I had a good run for a while, but you know, Pat, I didn't enjoy any of it."

What a shame he'd tried to fit into a counterculture he didn't like and had missed his chance to do something lasting. And what a shame he'd lost my trust years before in Malibu by suggesting a ménage à trois, which made me feel as if I were some anonymous female who'd wandered in off the street.

But it was too late to change that, and when he said he was applying for a teaching position at Western, I deliberately said, "A good idea. Send a writing sample."

Hannelore continued to fill her IWWG summer conferences with interesting writers, and another was Norah Vincent, who wrote the best-selling *Self-Made Man*.

Calling herself "a masculine-looking woman" who wore size 11½ shoes, Norah had decided to experiment with passing for a man, and she spent eighteen months disguised as "Ned" while she infiltrated male bowling leagues, male jobs, and such all-male bastions as lap-dancing parlors. When her book appeared, many reviewers lamented that after all the time she'd spent as a man, she'd ended up with clichés. They expressed the wish that she'd had deeper insights into males since she'd said, "Getting inside men's heads and out of my own was what this project was all about."

I wished I could have told the reviewers—and Norah herself—that the project was doomed from the start. She wasn't a man, and she still knew only what men said and did. Even after eighteen months, she still didn't know what truly lay inside their skulls and viscera. She was no better off pretending manhood than if she'd been one of the women in g-strings who observed—just as she did—what those men did and said.

But Norah hadn't been in my course at Skidmore, and since I tried not to grab people off the street and educate them, we'd merely sat side by side in one class and searched for each other's auras.

Possibly it was the guided imagery, or possibly Norah herself, but as we stared at each other darkly, I saw a pale green nimbus outlining her brunette hair. It was the only aura I've ever seen.

And I hadn't even noticed her feet.

My college chum Allene wrote that Jim Dickey had given an embarrassingly drunken reading at Rice and that at one point he read the notes the professor who'd introduced him had left on the podium. Jim had said in Colorado, "I make those Rice bastards pay plenty when they invite me to read," but since he'd been sinking ever deeper into alcohol over the years, I was glad I hadn't witnessed that last high-dollar reading.

And when I met Rosemary Daniell after Jim died, I was relieved that he and I hadn't seen each other again after Colorado.

He and Rosemary had apparently been lovers in the early 1960s, and in those years he obviously still had enough charisma to tell the old war stories and to elicit sympathy with tales of his shrewish wife, Maxine. He strove to make himself indispensable to the girls in his classes, and Rosemary said he often told her, "Keep working with me, baby, and you'll be a great writer."

According to her, he also insisted they have unprotected sex so he could father another baby. He added that he wouldn't acknowledge the child but that he'd send it an anonymous rose and a box of chocolates every birthday. Harry Hart mentions that episode in his biography of Jim, and it was easy to see the sentimental fantasy as one of Jim's inventions.

Rosemary shared her memories of Jim and asked if I'd slept with him, too. I couldn't quite say he'd never been my type, so I said, "I knew him in the early '50s. Back then he hadn't yet conquered his reluctance to sleep with students."

I thought about reassuring her that she was probably the first, but I didn't.

I won a First Stage Drama Award for writers who wanted to turn a piece of fiction into a one-act play. The prize was a week in Boston where actors coming to Emerson College would mount a staged reading of my *Grass Creek Chronicle*.

Six writers had received awards, and on the first day, I could tell that the stage manager, the dramaturge, and the director all liked my work. We went out to dinner, one actor went home to get me a sweatshirt since I hadn't brought warm enough clothes for a Boston spring, and I was convinced the experience would be rewarding.

The sixth winner didn't arrive until the second day, and when I came down to the dining room at the bed-and-breakfast, I saw a tall black woman with cornrows. She looked up from her baguette. "You one of the playwrights? I just got here." Of course we had breakfast together, and together we walked across the park to the theater.

"Who's that in the Civil War uniform?" she asked as we passed a statue.

"Robert Shaw. He commanded the black company that got slaughtered at the Battle of the Crater. Since he's prominent here in the park, Boston must be OK."

The minute we went into the auditorium, however, I realized how wrong I was.

The theater crew looked up and their expressions stiffened. The day before, they'd seen me. Now they obviously saw two black women. They avoided us in the audience during rehearsals, when we went for drinks afterward no one sat at our table—or invited us to sit with them—and no one mentioned lunch or dinner again.

We'd become as invisible in 1990s Boston as the blacks in 1950s Texas had been when I'd joined them.

The next year I got another award to turn a piece of fiction into a theater piece—the Judy and A.C. Greene Award from the Living Room Theatre in Salado, Texas— given to four writers who'd have a readers' theater production of their work. A final grand prize of fifteen hundred dollars would go to the author whose production most impressed the audiences and judges after the four presentations.

I sent pages from a manuscript of "Leaving Gilead," a novella set in Civil War Arkansas, which featured three characters: eight-year-old Saranell Birdsong, her mother, Geneva, and a male slave, Renny. When Raymond Carver of the theater group ("I'm the other Raymond Carver.") called to say my manuscript was one of the chosen four, he added, "I guess that means I have to find some black dude to play Renny."

I thought, Oh, brother, but all I said was, "I think you'll need some black dude."

Carver cast a lovely thirty-year-old actress as Geneva, a seventy-year-old actress who could beautifully slide into the voice of an eight-year-old, and as Renny, a black kid who worked at the nearest Walmart. When we entered the huge living room—able to hold an audience of a hundred as well as an indoor pool—naturally everyone but a couple of the kid's relatives was white.

He may or may not have felt uneasy in the wealthy setting, but even if he didn't, the bravado in his voice as he read my dialogue made the character of Renny come utterly alive. The exchanges between him, Saranell, and Geneva were electric, and the applause at the end echoed tumultuously over the actors and the heated pool.

The three-person ensemble, hands down, won the grand prize for me.

The glass case at the Civil War Prairie Grove Battle-field Museum held the pocket diary of a Union soldier lost on the field on December 8, 1862, and a transcript of the tiny inked script was on sale at the museum bookstore.

As I read the transcript, I could imagine the funny and charming man who considered the army—and the war it-self—a sardonic joke. He might have been another Samuel Clemens. And I conceived of a story that would have a twentieth-century woman discovering the little journal and falling in love with a soldier who'd been dead for nearly a century and a half.

But my second thought was that if the woman were a contemporary who lived at the edge of the grove the day of the battle, and if a wounded Yankee came to her porch and she let him in and bandaged him before she found the diary, then the story would be even more interesting, and the reader, too, could see and fall in love with the soldier.

My second version became "Diary of a Union Soldier," and *The Southern Review*, whose editors I no longer knew, brought it out in a commemorative issue. It was then an-thologized in a collection of Kentucky writers, in *Arkansas, Arkansas*, where I got to represent the Civil War, and at last in my collection of Civil War short fiction, *The Death of a Confederate Colonel*.

"Diary of a Union Soldier" became one of my prized stories, but it became Duane's all-time favorite, and every time he critiques a new story, he says, "Correct a couple of typos and this is ready to send. But it isn't quite 'Diary of a Union Soldier.'"

Barbara Kingsolver was invited to give a reading at Western Kentucky University. She still lived in Tucson, and after she was taxied in from the Nashville airport—only forty miles away and the closest airport to Bowling Green, Kentucky—we went out to lunch to catch up.

"I'm going to introduce you tonight. You want me to say anything in particular?"

She thought a second. "I guess I'd like you to talk about my three novels and my new nonfiction book." She smiled, and I guess she remembered how I'd talked about her at the IWWG conference. "Just don't say I'm a good kid."

"I can manage that."

Before the reading, the creative writing faculty took her to their favorite restaurant at the edge of town that served old-fashioned home cooking, family style. I was pretty sure she would have preferred vegetarian fare to the oversalted slices of ham, the crusted corn pone, and the overdone green beans and black-eyed peas, but neither of us said anything at the dinner or as Duane drove us back to campus in our pickup.

She was to read in the largest classroom in Cherry Hall, and I stood at the podium before our creative writing students and talked about her three novels and her new nonfiction book.

During the welcoming applause, when she wove through the desks, I saw that she wore her lucky red sneakers.

When she reached the front of the room I put an arm around her shoulders. "Oh, yes, I almost forgot. She's also a really good kid."

I got a writer's fellowship to the Château de Lavigny in Lausanne, Switzerland, and I decided to write a memoir of my years at Texas Southern.

Six international writers had been selected for the three-week stay, obligated only to give a brief reading of our work to a Swiss audience, and then have the freedom to write all day before we met for wine and dinner in the evenings.

But after the third day of retreating to my room to write, I realized that in every memoir I'd ever read, the narrator had a fierce struggle to overcome or a fierce reality to face. My Texas Southern experience didn't have either.

And the fourth morning when I went down to breakfast, and the two Frenchmen smiled and asked, "How is your work going?" I had to say, "The manuscript's crap." (Or maybe I said, *"merde."*)

I brought my café au lait to the table. "I may have to give it up."

"What is it about?"

"About the time I accidentally passed for black in the segregated South."

They gaped.

And when they asked for details, and I explained, they said, "That story is important. You must not quit. You must go finish it."

I sighed. "If you guys think so."

So with great effort and even more misgivings, I managed to complete a rough draft.

I came back from Switzerland with the completed draft, but Duane shook his head halfway through. A friend read it and bravely said, "This is a first. But I don't think this manuscript is any good."

And of course they were right.

I tried never to worry more than a day or two over rejection slips or failed projects—even narratives of two hundred pages—so I chucked the manuscript.

Then a week later, I realized I could use the material after all.

Twenty years before, I'd given a reading at a faltering Fayetteville bookstore whose owner had asked me to accept my honorarium in books, and one book I'd picked off the shelf was Scott Ellsworth's *Death in a Promised Land*, a history of the 1921 Tulsa riot/massacre. For two decades the white mob's destruction of Tulsa's black Greenwood area had festered in my mind. Given my point-of-view rule, I could never write the story the way it should be written—with a black protagonist caught in the riot. But suddenly, after the Château de Lavigny, I saw that I could use my own 1950s experience and put a white teacher, dark enough to be mistaken for black, in a Greenwood school.

I knew Tulsa, so I steeped myself in the 1920s, in the riot, and when I discovered that black soldiers from Tulsa had fought in World War I with the French after the American army refused them, I made my school principal a veteran. When I sent *If We Must Die* to Texas Christian University Press, the editors said if I'd change it to third person to keep the tension and let it come out as a young adult novel, they'd take it.

"How could you let this book come out as a young adult novel?

"That's the only slot TCU Press had."

"But a *children's* book!"

"Young adult isn't really children's literature," I said even as I remembered the woman in my creative writing course who'd become incensed and dropped the class after I suggested the novel she was working on about her teen years would make good young adult fiction. "But, hey, I don't care if the press wanted to bring it out as a coloring book. I think it's important to have my novel about the worst race riot in American history out there, and it *has* sold out the first edition."

"Well, I still think it should have come out as adult fiction. You're a literary writer. You don't need to write down for kids."

"I don't write down. I write the way I always do."

I didn't try to explain that I'm still out of sync with adult literary fiction and its cynical, cruel, and motiveless characters, its empty endings. But that with young adult fiction I might have a better chance of dealing with love and understanding and heroism.

And when I wrote *Border Ransom*, about the death of parents and 1914 El Paso and heroics in the Mexican Revolution with Pancho Villa, TCU Press didn't ask if I'd let it come out as young adult or if I'd change it to third person to maintain the suspense. They merely asked if I'd like to write a sequel.

I'd heard an agent say that if a writer published an autobiography, novel, nonfiction, or collection of short stories, she or he should publish three more before going on to something else. So I'd been telling Duane that whatever genre he was published in, he should stay with it. "Now that you've finished the book on Southern literature and Popular Press took it, don't you think you should write another? Every time we sit down for a wine, you come up with some new topic you could explore."

He looked at me across his wine glass. "I don't think I'm that interested in criticism any longer."

"You could always write another novel or another book of poems."

He shook his head. "I don't think so. I ran out of things I wanted to say in fiction and poetry, at least for the time being. I want to concentrate on music."

I knew music was his first love, that he heard melodies in his head, a sort of music of the spheres, which of course, I—with my near tone-deaf musical ability—couldn't hear, and I was glad he'd still been in English when I ran into him. If he'd been in a music department, I didn't think even Fate could have concocted a way to bring us together. I can't dance, I can't appreciate Mozart, and I knew I'd never respond to opera after the night in Rome when I'd gone to the Coliseum to hear *Aïda*. It was an outdoor production equipped with elephants and camels, but as I sat on the stone seats trying to listen, I nonetheless dozed off.

So I was glad we found each other over literature before he returned to a muse I couldn't follow.

"How do you become a writer, Dr. Carr?"

"Well, you have to want to write. If you don't want to write more than anything else, then you probably shouldn't do it."

The students around the seminar table waited, and I added, "Malcolm Gladwell says practice overcomes talent, that anyone who has devoted ten thousand hours to his craft can succeed. All you have to do is write a million words."

"O-o-o-e-e-e." It was a murmur of awe.

"It's not that much when you think about it. If each page has 250 words, two hundred pages is a 50,000-word book. To reach a million, you only need twenty books."

As I was saying it, I finally understood what my father meant when he warned me at fourteen that I couldn't make it as both a writer and a painter. I probably didn't have enough years to write twenty books and then paint for another ten thousand hours.

Later that evening as I clicked my wine glass to Duane's, I said, "But I like Gladwell. I never did believe in talent. I always thought that if anyone wrote as much and worked as hard at revising as I do, they'd have as many publications as I do."

"I know you've always thought that. But being good takes something else. Naturally a writer can't be conventional or hold anything back, he's got to be observant and honest, but he's also got to have understanding. That's the difference between being a hack and being good. And even *you* can't teach people to understand."

"I'm not sure."

"I am."

I realized I was looking through a glass milkily,
that I could no longer read street signs or recognize people
a few yards away, and when I went to the optometrist, he
said with practiced certainty, "Of course you need cataract
surgery."

So one eye at a time, I submitted to cataract surgery.

And suddenly, I no longer needed the occasional contacts or the glasses I'd depended on since I was eight. My
new vision was 20/20.

A few of my friends lamented the fact that I'd lost my
trademark horn-rimmed glasses. I still reached for phantom
glasses on the night table first thing in the morning and for
nonexistent glasses on my nose the last thing at night, but
for the first time in my life I could wear fashionable non-
prescription sunglasses and hoods that didn't flare out over
glasses' stems, and I could see.

But no one had told me about the colors.

Now I was also able to distinguish the crimson tracing
in the doctor's wallpaper, the brilliant ruby, emerald, and
topaz of streetlights, the blood-orange shades in unripe
persimmons, and the leaves of the forest beyond our pasture that flickered from chartreuse to evergreen to loden.
When I went out on our front porch, I could tell that the
Boston Mountains across the river were as purple as the
song insisted they should be, and I called back, "Duane
Carr, guess what?"

He came out to stand beside me, and I looked up at his
eyes, whose green I'd used for countless heroes in countless
stories and novels.

His eyes were Wedgwood blue.

I was giving a workshop in Albuquerque on my birthday, and the generic horoscope for the day said that in the coming year I'd get my heart's desire. I was pleased that millions of us born on March 13 across the world would get our heart's desire, but I had one problem. I had no idea what my unfulfilled desire was.

I had everything I'd ever conceived of wanting. I had a person with whom I could spend twenty-four hours a day and still look forward to our afternoon Chardonnay; I had published books; I had four children who graduated from college, married—or didn't—had children—or didn't—whom I loved unconditionally; I had close friends to whom I'd trust my life; I had a new book, *The Death of a Confederate Colonel*, win three fiction prizes; and I had a former student take my novel, *If We Must Die*, to Hollywood to see about getting it made into a film.

Maybe with all that good fortune, I just needed to know I'd become a writer.

And perhaps my heart's desire was merely the chance to keep writing.

Afterword

Once at a party, an amateur psychic was going around the room reading palms. When she looked in my hand, she said, "Good Lord. There are a thousand people in here."

I haven't used them all.

But I did change a few names, omit a few, and leave out occasional surnames for anonymity. Some people didn't merit a page, some were too important for a page, with some I had no conflict and hence no narrative resolution—as Jennifer says, "I guess that's a compliment"—and some who appear on the periphery of this story actually make up the core of my being (particularly my children, whose rare appearances belie the fact that—as I once thought while watching a plane take off with them—"There goes my life.").

I tried not to invent myself, tried to be true to events, tried not to harm or embarrass anyone. But of course memory is always fallible, always part fiction.